IT'S
SPORTS QUIZ TIME...
NOSTALGICALLY
REMEMBERED...

That is, *some* of you will remember. Others not ancient enough will have read or heard about these sports figures and events from the past and not so far past. It's the greatest quiz book yet, devoted to all sports—famed athletes, loved and unloved; those who won, those who lost; where played and when; scores, freaky events, trophies, money awarded, crazy names, curious quirks, and other happenings in stadiums, courts, alleys; sporting events on land, sea, and in the air! The quizzes in this book make a great *new* sport—you'll be playing SPORTS NOSTALGIA QUIZ off the field, at home, in the clubhouse, between innings, beers, brawls, during rainouts and blackouts (bring flashlight!)

Whatever, you're going to have a whale of a time!

Super Football Books from SIGNET

The Sports Nostalgia Quiz Book

Zander Hollander
and
David Schulz

AN ASSOCIATED FEATURES BOOK

A SIGNET BOOK

NEW AMERICAN LIBRARY

SIGNET, SIGNET CLASSIC, MENTOR, PLUME, MERIDIAN AND NAL BOOKS
are published by New American Library,
1633 Broadway, New York, New York 10019

FIRST PRINTING, FEBRUARY, 1975

FIRST PRINTING (REVISED AND UPDATED EDITION), OCTOBER, 1985

1 2 3 4 5 6 7 8 9

PRINTED IN THE UNITED STATES OF AMERICA

Contents

(Numbers refer to quizzes, not pages)

Introduction

Let's start with a quiz. What does Gorgeous George have in common with Joe DiMaggio? Wilt Chamberlain with Ring Lardner? Jack Dempsey with Tarzan? Duke Snider with Willie Hoppe? Rocket Richard with Cornelius McGillicuddy? Bill Tilden with the Galloping Ghost? Sonja Henie with Frank Filchock? Clem McCarthy with Chuck Connors? Hank Luisetti with Gordie Howe? Sammy Baugh with Mickey Owens? Jesse Owens with Don Carter? A. J. Foyt with Glenn Cunningham? Whizzer White with Hurry-Up Yost?

The answer: they're all to be found in a cast of hundreds, if not thousands, in the revised and updated *The Sports Nostalgia Quiz Book*—a book crammed with games to be played off the field, in the clubhouse, between innings, beers, and brawls, during rainouts and blackouts (with candle).

This is all the world of recall and replay, fun and sports division, and the only tricks that will be played here are by your memory.

A quiz book offers a unique way of writing about the past—the big names, tht outstanding events, the significant dates, the unusual outcomes—as questions, answers, or clues. From the Olympic Games to the Rose Bowl, from the muffed ball to the oddball, from the America's Cup to the Stanley Cup, from the Splendid Splinter to the Brown Bomber—you'll find 1,492 questions in more than 150 quizzes.

Each quiz has a number, and the answers are under the corresponding numbers in the Answer Section in the back of the book.

Climb aboard and ride the Iron Horse or Whirlaway, swim the English Channel, join the Kraut Line, cheer, cheer for Knute Rockne and old Notre Dame, make way for a couple of Babes—Ruth and Didrikson—see flicks like *Fear Strikes Out* and *Monkey on My Back,* and when the going gets tough, remember to hit 'em where they . . . oops, you'll have to look it up.

1. NFL Names of Fame

Who were

1. The Galloping Ghost
2. The Horse
3. Automatic Jack
4. The Toe
5. Deacon Dan
6. The Little General
7. Big Daddy
8. Night Train
9. Johnny Blood
10. The Dutchman

2. Baseball's One of a Kind

Some nicknames are common to baseball, such as Lefty or Red, while others are so distinctive they immediately bring to mind only one player, even if he played so long ago that there are few people alive who saw him play. Identify

1. The Beast
2. The Rajah
3. The Tiger
4. The Kid
5. The Bambino
6. The Cat

7. The Kitten
8. The Hat
9. The Lip
10. The Old Fox
11. The Splendid Splinter
12. The Fordham Flash
13. The Man
14. The Grand Old Man
15. The Trojan
16. The Iron Horse
17. The Reading Rifle
18. The Golden Greek
19. The Duke of Tralee
20. The Pride of Havana
21. The Little Professor

3. Presidents in Sport

1. This energetic President played on his college freshman and junior varsity football teams; the freshman golf and swimming teams, and represented his school in sailing competition. Name him.

2. Who was the President who tried his hand at coaching athletic teams while teaching history at Wesleyan?

3. Which President once played football against Jim Thorpe?

4. The President who threw out the "first ball" on baseball's opening day in 1910 also was a wrestler and rowed stroke at Yale. Name him.

5. A self-proclaimed "nation's No.-1 football fan," this President was a bench-warmer on his college football team. Name him.

4. Locate the Bowl

It all started with the Rose Bowl at the turn of the century, and by now there have been more than fifty different "bowl" games played by various collegiate and amateur teams. Match the name of the bowl to the city in which it is, or was, located.

1.	Sugar Bowl	a)	New Orleans, La.
2.	Liberty Bowl	b)	New York, N.Y.
3.	Bluebonnet Bowl	c)	Mobile, Ala.
4.	Sun Bowl	d)	Dallas, Tex.
5.	Missile Bowl	e)	Allentown, Pa.
6.	Boardwalk Bowl	f)	Sacramento, Calif.
7.	Grantland Rice Bowl	g)	Excelsior Springs, Mo.
8.	Pecan Bowl	h)	Oklahoma City, Okla.
9.	Rose Bowl	i)	Atlantic City, N.J.
10.	All-Sports Bowl	j)	Jacksonville, Fla.
11.	Orange Bowl	k)	Honolulu, Hawaii
12.	Gotham Bowl	l)	Murfreesboro, Tenn.
13.	Cement Bowl	m)	Houston, Tex.
14.	Peach Bowl	n)	Brunswick, Ga.
15.	Cotton Bowl	o)	Miami, Fla.
16.	Camelia Bowl	p)	Pasadena, Calif.
17.	Hula Bowl	q)	El Paso, Tex.
18.	Mineral Bowl	r)	Memphis, Tenn.
19.	Senior Bowl	s)	Atlanta, Ga.
20.	Gator Bowl	t)	Abilene, Tex.
21.	Golden Isles Bowl	u)	Orlando, Fla.

5. Off the Boards

1. The first year the NBA kept records on rebounding was 1951. What Syracuse player led the league that season with 1,080?

2. What Seton Hall player holds the NCAA record for most rebounds in a single season with 734?

3. What Kentucky State player holds the all-time rebound record with 799?

4. What is the NBA record for most rebounds in a game, and who holds it?

5. What LaSalle player holds the four-year career rebound record for major college players?

6. Wilt Chamberlain and Bill Russell account for 22 of the 24 times one man has grabbed 40 or more rebounds in a regular season NBA game. Who were the other two men to do it?

7. In 1956, a 6-5 center from Marshall established a collegiate single-season record for rebounding average that still stands today. Who is he?

8. The 1960-61 Detroit Pistons were the first team to have two men with more than 1000 rebounds each in the same season. Who were they?

9. The NCAA began keeping rebounding statistics in 1951. W at 6-1 player from Penn won the first NCAA rebounding title?

10. Only one player from the Rochester-Cincinnati-Kansas City franchise ever led the NBA in rebounding. Name him.

6. Hockey Combinations

1. In 1963-64, Chicago placed five men on the All-Star team. Name them.

2. Name the four Boucher brothers who played in the NHL.

3. What outstanding defenseman was moved to right wing to play on Boston's Dynamite Line with Cooney Weiland and Dutch Gainor?

4. Name the Boston line that scored 336 points in 1970-71.

5. In 1944-45, five of the first team All-Stars were Montreal Canadiens. Who was the lone outsider?

6. Who was on the 1944-45 Montreal line with Maurice Richard when he scored 50 goals?

7. Who was the center on the New York Ranger line with the Cook brothers, Bill and Bun?

8. Who replaced Sid Abel on Detroit's Production Line with Gordie Howe and Ted Lindsay?

9. Who was the right wing on the Chicago line with Max and Doug Bentley?

10. With Larry Aurie and Herbie Lewis on the wings, who was the center on this Detroit line of the 1930s?

7. One Man on a Horse

Great races are a combination of the right horse trained properly and an outstanding jockey riding. Match the following jockeys with their winning mounts in Triple Crown races.

1. Eddie Arcaro	a) Cannonero
2. Johnny Sellers	b) Tim Tam
3. Bill Shoemaker	c) Citation
4. Ron Turcotte	d) Count Fleet
5. Manny Ycaza	e) Chateaugay
6. Braulio Baeza	f) Pensive
7. Bill Hartack	g) Secretariat
8. Johnny Longden	h) Needles
9. Earl Sande	i) Capot
10. Gustavo Avila	j) Count Fleet
11. Ishmael Valenzuela	k) Kauai King
12. Dave Erb	l) Carry Back
13. Ted Atkinson	m) Quadrangle
14. Don Brumfield	n) Northern Dancer
15. Conn McCreary	o) Swaps

8. Molders of Men

Professional sports may have their dynasties built around a star or a group of players, but at the college level any dynasty must necessarily center on the genius of the head coach. Match these football coaches with the colleges with which they are most closely identified.

1. Red Blaik
2. Jess Neely
3. Amos Alonzo Stag
4. Knute Rockne
5. Pop Warner
6. Red Sanders
7. Dutch Meyer
8. Ben Schwartzwalder
9. Bud Wilkenson
10. Eddie Erdelatz
11. Jock Sutherland
12. Fielding "Hurry-Up" Yost
13. Andy Gustafson
14. Bobby Dodd
15. Alonzo Gaither
16. Bob Zuppke
17. Lou Little
18. Johnny Vaught
19. Warren Woodson
20. Paul "Tony" Hinkle
21. Darrell Royal
22. Eddie Robinson

a) Texas
b) Oklahoma
c) Syracuse
d) New Mexico State
e) Army
f) Florida A&M
g) Chicago
h) Grambling
i) Notre Dame
j) Butler
k) Georgia Tech
l) Rice

m) Mississippi
n) Stanford
o) UCLA
p) Columbia
q) Texas Christian
r) Navy
s) Pittsburgh
t) Illinois
u) Michigan
v) Miami (Fla.)

9. The Masters

1. Who won the first Masters golf tournament by a single stroke over Craig Wood in 1934?

2. Who lost a three-way playoff in 1966 but came back to win the 1967 Masters?

3. Who was the amateur, who later turned professional, who finished a stroke behind Jack Burke in the 1956 Masters?

4. Who shot a course-sizzling 65 in the second round en route to a seven-stroke victory in 1955?

5. Who was the amateur who tied with Byron Nelson, two strokes behind winner Jimmy Demaret in 1947?

6. Who shot a record 271 on the Augusta National Course in 1965 to finish nine strokes ahead of Arnold Palmer and Gary Player?

7. What 1966 Masters winner failed to make the 36-hole cut in 1967?

8. The 1957 winner of the Masters predicted—two weeks before the event—that not only would he win, but that he would shoot a 283, which he did. Who was he?

9. In 1942, Ben Hogan made up three strokes on the final round to tie the leader. Then he went three strokes up in the playoff round, but still lost by two. Who beat him?

10. Sam Snead defeated Ben Hogan, 70-71, in a playoff to win in 1954; but name the amateur who made headlines by leading after 36 holes, canning a hole-in-one and finishing only a stroke off the leaders.

10. Tarzan

Name these famous Tarzans:

1. The one-time Los Angeles Ram linebacker who played Tarzan in the late 1960s.

2. A swimmer named Clarence who played Tarzan before moving to other movie roles.

3. The most famous Tarzan, an Olympic gold medalist in 1924 and 1928.

4. The Olympic decathlon winner of 1936 who was also a movie Tarzan.

5. The Villanova pole-vaulter called Tarzan because he wanted to play the role in films.

11. Carom Crown

Which of these men never led the NBA in rebounds?

    a) Neil Johnston
    b) Maurice Stokes
    c) Clyde Lovellette

12. Women Olympians

Match these female Olympic medal winners with the events in which they won their gold.

1.	Wilma Rudolph	a)	Shot put
2.	Helen Stephens	b)	200 meters
3.	Tamara Press	c)	800 meters
4.	Mary Rand	d)	Discus
5.	Edith McGuire	e)	100 meters
6.	Babe Didrikson	f)	High jump
7.	Betty Cuthbert	g)	400-meter relay
8.	Lillian Copeland	h)	Long jump
9.	Jean Shiley	i)	400 meters
10.	Madeline Manning	j)	80-meter hurdles

13. America's Cup

1. Name the skipper, who also served as President Nixon's Chief of Protocol, who successfully defended the America's Cup aboard *Weatherly* and *Intrepid* in 1962 and 1967.

2. What Englishman with a famous aviation name skippered *Endeavor* to two victories in the 1934 series before losing to the American defender?

3. How many times did Sir Thomas Lipton try, and fail, to win the America's Cup?

4. How did the Cup get its name?

5. Only one other country in addition to Australia, 1983 Cup winner, and England has challenged the U.S. in the Cup finals? Name the country.

6. *Enterprise* in 1930, *Rainbow* in 1934, and *Ranger* in 1937 were all successful defenders of the Cup, and all were skippered by the same man. Name him.

14. Netmen

1. What 1939 Wimbledon singles champion was making money playing tennis thirty-five years later?

2. Only two men have won tennis' "grand slam," the championships in the U.S., Australia, France, and Wimbledon. Name them.

3. It took a record seventy games to decide the men's doubles championship in 1968 at Wimbledon. Name the four Australians involved.

4. What American was ranked No.-1 professional in the world for eight straight years (1954-61)?

5. Who won the U.S. singles title in six consecutive years (1920-25)?

6. It was February 16, 1968, and the event was the U.S. Indoor Men's Doubles Championships. Mark Cox and Robert Wilson of Great Britain won, 26-24, 17-19, 30-28. Who were the tenacious losers from the U.S.?

7. What American was the youngest man to win the Wimbledon title when, at seventeen, he and Rafael Osuna took the doubles championship in 1960?

8. Who is the American player of the 1940s who never lost a singles match in Davis Cup competition?

9. Professionals were allowed to play in the U.S. Nationals for the first time in 1968, but an amateur still won the singles title. Name the man who beat Tom Okker that year.

10. Who headed the 1937 U.S. Davis Cup team that defeated Nazi Germany and England to win the Cup for America for the first time in a decade?

15. Wedding of Sports

Match the athletes who became man and wife.

1. Ralph Kiner (baseball)
2. Jack Kelly (sculls)
3. Donald Brinker (pentathlon)
4. Jackie Jensen (baseball)
5. Harold Connolly (track and field)

a) Zoe Ann Olson (diving)
b) Olga Fikotova (track and field)
c) Nancy Chaffee (tennis)
d) Mary Freeman (swimming)
e) Maureen Connolly (tennis)

16. On the Move

Professional teams change locations more quickly than most people can keep track. Match the teams with the city or state that was once—but no longer is—home.

1. Boston	a) Bulldogs
2. Anaheim	b) Stars
3. Seattle	c) Olympians
4. Houston	d) Rockets
5. New Jersey	e) Steamrollers
6. Rochester	f) Condors
7. Chicago	g) Blackhawks
8. New Orleans	h) Browns
9. Dallas	i) Mavericks
10. St. Louis	j) Hawks
11. Syracuse	k) Amigos
12. Tri-Cities	l) Athletics
13. Oakland	m) Pilots
14. Washington	n) Nationals
15. Indianapolis	o) Pistons
16. Los Angeles	p) Muskies
17. Philadelphia	q) Americans
18. Providence	r) Zephyrs
19. Cleveland	s) Caps
20. San Diego	t) Rams
21. Minnesota	u) Lakers
22. Minneapolis	v) Buccaneers
23. New York	w) Royals
24. Pittsburgh	x) Pros
25. Milwaukee	y) Braves
26. Memphis	z) Oaks
27. Fort Wayne	zz) Chaparrals

17. The Brown Bomber

1. Joe Louis held the heavyweight championship longer than any other man. How long was that?

2. Whom did Louis beat for the title? When? Where?

3. How did Louis' reign end? When?

4. How many times did Louis defend his crown?

5. Louis beat five challengers twice each. Name them.

6. What did Gus Dorazio and Tony Musto have to do with Louis?

7. Where was Louis born?

8. Who beat Louis in his comeback bid?

9. In which of these cities did Louis not make a title defense: San Francisco, Detroit, Washington, St. Louis, Los Angeles?

10. Who was the referee in twelve of Louis' title fights?

18. The Sullivan Award

1. Who was the swimmer who was the first woman to receive the Sullivan Trophy in 1944?

2. Only two basketball players have been awarded the trophy. Name them.

3. Even though it was not an Olympic year, this decathlon performer was honored in 1969. Name him.

4. In 1933 and 1934, two milers who frequently competed against each other received the award. Name them.

5. The only figure skater to do so won the honor in 1949. Who was it?

6. In 1961, she became the first woman track performer to gain Sullivan honors. Name her.

7. What world-record-breaking pole-vaulter won the trophy in 1942?

8. Who was the last golfer to win the award?

9. Mark Spitz was honored in 1971 and couldn't repeat in 1972 despite his seven Olympic medals in Munich. Who won in 1972?

10. Only one tennis player has received the Sullivan Trophy. Who?

19. Boners

1. In 1926, who was the Brooklyn Dodger who "tripled" into a double play by being caught on third base with two other runners?

2. What Milwaukee pitcher committed 2 errors while covering first base, enabling the Yankees to win the 1958 World Series?

3. Who was the Cincinnati catcher who blocked an errant pitch with his body and then couldn't find the ball—only three feet away—while two Yankees scored in the 10th inning of a 1939 World Series game?

4. Who was the New York first baseman who committed a three-base error in the 1963 World Series to set up a Dodger run which helped Los Angeles sweep a four-game Series?

5. Who made the boner—failing to touch second base on a teammate's single—that cost the Giants a late-season victory and the 1908 pennant?

6. What Dodger catcher missed holding on to a third strike which allowed Tommy Henrich to reach first base safely and opened the way for a Yankee World Series victory in 1941?

7. Who was the Chicago Cub pitcher who threw Babe Ruth a home run ball after the Bambino had taken two strikes and pointed to the spot over the Wrigley Field fence where he would hit the ball in the 1932 World Series?

20. Running Wild

1. Jim Brown led the NFL in rushing eight times. Name the only other men who were able to lead the league in rushing as many as four times.

2. Whose 3-yard run for a Notre Dame touchdown ended Oklahoma's 47-game winning streak in 1957.

3. What Chicago Cardinal ran for a record 6 touchdowns against the Bears on November 28, 1929?

4. What NFL star scored 60 touchdowns in his varsity days at a small school between 1946 and 1949, a record that still stands today?

5. Who scored more touchdowns in NFL championship games, Super Bowl or otherwise, than any other player?

6. What All-American ended his regular-season collegiate career in 1956 by scoring 6 touchdowns and 7 extra points against Colgate?

7. Even with All-America passer Johnny Lujack in the backfield, Notre Dame's 1948 team rolled up 3194 yards rushing. Who were the two main ball-carriers for the Irish?

8. Who was the first runner in NFL history to gain 200 yards in a single game when he carried for 215 against the Giants on October 18, 1933?

9. In 1959, 1960, and 1961, New Mexico State had runners who led the nation in both rushing and scoring. Name the three Aggies who accomplished this.

10. What Cleveland Brown fullback averaged more than 17 yards a carry in eleven attempts in a game against Pittsburgh in 1950?

21. Bomb Squad

1. Whose shot from beyond midcourt—enabling Rhode Island to tie Bowling Green at the end of regulation time—was the most stunning play of the 1946 NIT?

2. Who was the Alabama player who made a shot 84 feet, 11 inches from the basket against North Carolina during the 1954-55 season?

3. Who holds the ABA record for most long-range, 3-point goals attempted (26) and made (10) in a single game?

4. What Kentucky Colonel guard made seven 3-point goals in seven attempts in a 1968 ABA game?

5. Who made the 65-foot, last-second shot that sent the NBA championship series game between Los Angeles and New York into overtime in 1970?

22. Court Order

Which of these men never led the NBA in assists?

    a) Dick McGuire
    b) Guy Rodgers
    c) Slater Martin

23. NHL All-Stars

1. Who has played in more NHL All-Star Games than any other man?

2. Who has scored the most goals in one All-Star Game?

3. What Chicago Black Hawk holds the record for most penalties in a single period of an All-Star Game?

4. What New York Ranger scored 2 goals within 1:19 in the 1953 classic?

5. What goalie has appeared in the most All-Star Games?

6. What has been the highest-scoring All-Star Game?

7. Who are the five players who have scored the most points (4) in an All-Star Game?

8. Who was the Vancouver forward who scored two goals in an All-Star Game record 10 seconds in 1976?

9. What Edmonton forward had three assists in one period for an All-Star Game record in 1983?

10. Who was the goaltender for the All-Stars when Toronto scored 4 goals in the opening period for a 4-1 victory in 1962?

24. Complete the Quote

1. Playing a tie game is like . . .
2. When the going gets tough . . .
3. Nice guys . . .
4. Take two and . . .
5. It's not whether you win or lose . . .
6. They put their pants on . . .
7. We play them one game . . .
8. The game is never over . . .
9. A punt, a pass, and . . .
10. Hit 'em where . . .
11. Good field . . .

25. The Indy 500

1. Who was the first three-time winner of the race?

2. Ray Harroun won the first 500 in 1911 with what average speed?

3. Who was the first foreign driver to win at Indianapolis, in 1965?

4. What was the name of the Offenhauser engine before Fred Offenhauser acquired the rights to it?

5. Wilbur Shaw was the first to win consecutive 500s, when he did it in 1939 and 1940. Who was the second?

6. What type of car did Shaw drive in his consecutive victories?

7. What kind of car did Jimmy Clark drive to victory in 1965?

8. What German-named engine powered Jimmy Murphy's winning racer in 1922?

9. Who set a one-lap qualifying time record with 171.953 miles per hour in a turbine-powered Lotus in 1968?

10. Who was the first driver to win in one of Andy Granatelli's STP Specials?

26. Iron Men

1. Who was the Marshall College product who joined the Syracuse Nationals in 1958 and went on to establish an NBA record for most games played (with 1122)?

2. Playing for Iowa in 1939, this Iron Man played 402 out of a possible 420 minutes, handling the kicking chores and playing a part in 107 of the Hawkeyes' 135 points during the season. Name him.

3. Who is the hockey player who appeared in 630 consecutive games—nine 70-game seasons—with the New York Rangers and Boston Bruins between 1955 and 1964?

4. The Iron Horse, Lou Gehrig, set the major league record by playing in 2,130 consecutive games. Who holds the National League record of 1,207?

5. Though the era of two-way football was long gone, this Philadelphia Eagle played center and linebacker in leading his team to a 17-13 victory over Green Bay in the 1960 NFL championship game. Name him.

6. Despite the rigors of one-night stands in the NBA, this man played in 844 consecutive regular season games between 1954 and 1965 with Syracuse, Philadelphia, and Baltimore. Name him.

7. Who was the tennis pro who at the age of forty-one played in a match that lasted more than five hours in 1965 and defeated Charles Pasarell, 22-24, 1-6, 16-14, 6-3, 11-9?

8. The American League record for innings pitched in a career is 5924 while the National League mark is 5246. Who are the respective record-holders?

9. Who was the back-up quarterback for the Chicago Bears in 1949 who was still playing professionally a quarter of a century later?

10. Pete Rose holds the major league and National League record for most games played in a career and Carl Yastrzemski set the American League standard. Whose records did they break?

27. Basketball Firsts

1. Which was the only team to win both the NIT and NCAA tournaments in the same year?

2. Who won the first NCAA championship game in 1939?

3. Which came first, the NIT or the NCAA post-season tournament?

4. Which was the first major college to average more than 100 points a game for a season?

5. Who played in the first basketball game ever televised?

6. The first time the winner of the NCAA tournament met the winner of the NIT in a playoff was in 1943. Name the teams and winner of this Red Cross benefit game.

7. Which was the first West Coast team to win the NIT?

8. Which was the first New England school to win the NCAA championship?

9. What school won the first nationally-televised NCAA championship game in 1954?

10. Which was the first independent school to win the NCAA tournament?

28. Breaking the Color Line

1. Who was the first black to win the Heisman Trophy as the outstanding college football player of the year?

2. What American Basketball League team had the first black head coach in big-time professional basketball?

3. Who was the first black to win a tennis championship at Wimbledon?

4. Who were the first black basketball players in the NBA?

5. Who was the first black to play on the official PGA golf tour?

6. Who was the first black to carry the American flag in the Olympic ceremonies when he did so in Rome in 1960?

7. Who was the first black baseball player in the American League?

8. Who was the first black man to win the U.S. National singles title?

9. Who was the first black to be the head coach of an NFL team?

29. Winter Sports

1. Who was the U.S. men's downhill skiing champion in 1957 and 1959 who was killed in an avalanche shortly after the 1964 Winter Olympics?

2. World Cup skiing competition was instituted in 1967. Who won the first two men's titles?

3. What two American women won three medals skiing for the U.S.—more than any other country—in the 1960 Winter Olympics at Squaw Valley?

4. Who was the Norwegian-born ski jumper who set several records in the United States, winning 42 of 48 tournaments in which he was entered? He was killed in Italy serving with the U.S. Army Ski Patrol during World War II.

5. What Canadian woman dominated downhill skiing world-class competition in the late 1960s?

30. Schools for Kicking

Name the colleges these professional kickers attended.

1. Lou Groza	a) Cornell
2. Pat Summerall	b) Texas A&M
3. Paul Hornung	c) Florida
4. Pat Harder	d) Southern Mississippi
5. Don Chandler	e) Princeton
6. Bert Rechichar	f) New Mexico
7. Tommy Davis	g) Upper Iowa
8. Ben Agajanian	h) Adams State
9. Gordy Soltau	i) Oregon State
10. Sam Baker	j) New Mexico State
11. Mike Eischeid	k) Tennessee
12. Don Cockcroft	l) Minnesota
13. Jerrel Wilson	m) Georgia
14. Danny Villanueva	n) UCLA
15. Yale Lary	o) Wisconsin
16. Charley Gogolak	p) Arkansas
17. Pete Gogolak	q) Louisiana State
18. Bobby Walston	r) Notre Dame
19. Bob Waterfield	s) Ohio State

31. Amateur Golfers

1. Who won five U.S. men's amateur titles, more than anyone else?

2. Who shot a 30 for nine holes during the 1932 U.S. amateur tournament?

3. Who was the oldest man ever to win the U.S. amateur title?

4. Jack Nicklaus won the U.S. amateur championship in 1959 and 1961. Who won it in 1960?

5. Only one amateur has won a U.S. Women's Open. Name her.

6. Who is the only American to win the U.S., British, and Canadian amateur titles?

7. Who won the most women's amateur championships (six)?

8. What American shot a 29 for nine holes in the 1948 British Amateur Championships at Sandwich?

9. What U.S. golfer and singer won the Canadian amateur in 1953?

10. Who was the last amateur to win the U.S. Men's Open?

32. Table Games

1. Who was the eighteen-year-old billiards player who beat world champion Maurice Vignaux in 1906, the first of fifty-one championships for him?

2. This man won his first national amateur three-cushion billiards championship in 1931, his last in 1964, winning the title eighteen times in all. He was also the world champion in 1936.

3. Who was the man whose father had been a champion before him and was one of the top billiards competitors of the 1920s and '30s?

4. Considered one of the greatest pocket billiard players of all time, he held the world professional championship nineteen times between 1919 and 1937. Who is he?

5. Between 1926 and 1946, who held the world professional three-cushion billiard championship seven times and set several records in 18.1-balkline competition?

6. Who was thirteen times pocket billiards champion between 1941 and 1956?

33. Hardwood Pointers

Which of these men never led the NBA in scoring?

a) Jack Twyman
b) Paul Arizin
c) George Yardley

34. Hockey Hall of Fame

Who is

1. The forward-defenseman who scored 200 goals in his career with the Ottawa Senators, Montreal Maroons, and New York Americans between 1924 and 1941?

2. The center who played on eleven Stanley Cup champions in his twenty years in the NHL?

3. The Maple Leaf center who won the first Calder Trophy in 1936-37 and played his entire career with Toronto?

4. The man who starred with Seattle and Victoria in the old Pacific Coast Hockey League as well as with Detroit in the NHL and is credited with originating the hook check?

5. The goalie who registered 22 shutouts during the 44-game NHL schedule in 1928-29 with the Montreal Canadiens?

6. The deft stickhandler who played center for Chicago and Detroit, earning league Most Valuable Player honors for the 1945-46 season?

7. The forward who set the career goal-scoring mark that Maurice Richard broke?

8. The man who spent 13½ seasons with Boston and is considered one of the greatest defensemen of all time?

9. The New York Ranger center who won the Lady Byng Trophy for sportsmanship seven times?

10. The goalie, called Mr. Zero, who was one of the first American-born stars of the NHL?

35. Home Run Pitches

1. Who threw Bobby Thomson the home run that won the 1951 pennant for the Giants?

2. What Washington Senator threw Babe Ruth's No. 60 in 1927?

3. What American League refugee threw Henry Aaron's first home run in the major leagues?

4. Who threw Roger Maris the home run ball in 1961 that broke Babe Ruth's single-season record?

5. Willie Mays is the third leading home run hitter of all time. Who threw him his first home run in 1951?

36. Scribes

Match these former sportswriters with the literary works associated with them.

1. Westbrook Pegler
2. Paul Gallico
3. Jimmy Breslin

4. Ring Lardner
5. Damon Runyon

a) *You Know Me, Al*
b) *Guys and Dolls*
c) *George Spelvin, American*
d) *Snow Goose*
e) *The Gang That Couldn't Shoot Straight*

37. Rose Bowl

1. The only time the Rose Bowl was played outside of Southern California was in 1942 because of wartime restrictions. Oregon played whom, and where?

2. Earl "Greasy" Neale was the coach, and he used only eleven players during the entire game as his team held powerful California to a scoreless tie in the 1922 Rose Bowl. Name his team.

3. Northwestern has been to the Rose Bowl only once, in 1949, when the Wildcats beat California, 20-14. Who was the Northwestern halfback selected as the game's outstanding player?

4. Which was the first Southern team to play in the Rose Bowl?

5. Who were the quarterback and end combination from Wisconsin that broke all sorts of records in the 1963 Rose Bowl, but to no avail as Southern California won, 42-37?

6. Only once have two Pacific Coast teams played in the Rose Bowl (in 1944). Name the teams and the winner.

7. Who was the All-American rollout quarterback who led Minnesota to a 21-3 victory over UCLA in 1962?

8. Big Ten teams had won six straight games until Southern California beat Wisconsin, 7-0, in 1952. Who scored the Trojan touchdown?

9. In 1960 and 1961, Washington became the first team to beat Big Ten representatives in back-to-back games. Who was the Huskies' quarterback who sparked the victories?

38. All-America Basketball

1. The first Associated Press All-America basketball selections were made in 1948, for the 1947-48 season. Name five who made the team.

2. Indiana was ranked No. 1 and won the NCAA tourney in 1953, yet didn't have an All-America player. What five were named?

3. Only four Ivy League players have been named to All-America teams since World War II. Name them.

4. Name the three men on the 1948-49 Kentucky team who were All-Americans.

5. Name three West Virginia players who were named to All-America teams in the 1950s.

6. CCNY won both the NIT and NCAA in 1950, yet didn't have one All-America player. Name the men who made the team.

7. Wilt Chamberlain, Oscar Robertson, and Elgin Baylor were the big men on the 1958 All-America team. Who were the "little men"?

8. Two 1954 All-Americans would later play together with the St. Louis Hawks as two-thirds of "the Untouchables." Name them.

9. What "Owl without a vowel" was a 1951 All-American?

10. The 1965-66 season represents a gap in UCLA's string of NCAA championships. Likewise, the Bruins had no All-America players that season. Name the five Associated Press selections.

39. Down Memory Lane

1. Who was the first million-dollar winner on the Professional Bowlers Association tour?

2. What Hall of Famer, who won the All-Star singles tournament in 1956, was the first man to bowl a 300-game on television?

3. Billy Golembiewski won the Masters Championship in 1960 and 1962. Who was the 1961 winner?

4. Who was the woman bowler of the year in both 1968 and 1969?

5. Who is the Hall of Famer who bowled the first 300-game in American Bowling Congress tournament history in 1913, and who also won the all-events title in 1929 with 2019, a score that stood for ten years?

6. Who was the Southerner whose twenty-year tournament average was 202 while bowling with championship teams in 1949, 1952, 1953, and 1955.

7. Who won the first Bowling Proprietors Association of America Women's All-Star singles titles in 1949 and 1950?

8. What touring professional once bowled a record 34 strikes in a three-game series for a score of 869?

9. What professional had a 212.1 tour average in 1966, when he was selected everybody's pro bowler of the year?

10. Who was the woman bowler who beat champion Jimmy Smith, 740-687, in a match in her hometown of Pueblo, Colorado, in 1926?

40. Out of Their League

Many players are noted for their achievements in only one sport, but could just as easily have been remem-

bered for prowess in some other field of endeavor. Fill in the blanks.

1. Byron "Whizzer" White is known for his exploits on the football field, but he was also a star at Colorado in ————.

2. Golfer Jack Nicklaus could have had a career in ———— since he was a standout on his college team.

3. Jackie Robinson is in baseball's Hall of Fame, but while attending UCLA he also excelled in ————.

4. Alvin Dark was a major league shortstop all the way, but at Louisiana State he is best remembered for ————.

5. The Kansas City Chiefs' Curly Culp was a ferocious lineman, but in college at Arizona State he was a standout ————.

6. Pittsburgh shortstop Dick Groat was a star of a different sort at Duke in ————.

7. Texas A&M shotputter Randy Matson was drafted by the professionals in ————.

8. Ken "Hawk" Harrelson was a high school football star, but he quit baseball to become ————.

9. When New York Jet lineman Winston Hill was in college, he was captain of the school's ———— team.

10. Greasy Neale is associated with football as one of the all-time great coaches, but he also made money as a ————.

41. Grappling with Greatness

1. Who was the wrestler who wore marcelled hair, velvet robes, and had his valet sprinkle the ring, the ref, and his opponents with perfume?

2. With former champion Strangler Lewis as his manager, who was the wrestler regarded as heavyweight champion in the late 1940s and early 1950s?

3. What wrestler wore his monocle into the ring and was always followed by his trusty valet?

4. What wrestler of Italian extraction who worked in bare feet popularized the flying dropkick?

5. What NFL defensive linemen and teammates were also wrestling partners in tag-team matches?

6. Who was the blond wrestler with the "Mr. America" build who was born Eugene Zygowicz in Chicago in 1925?

7. A former boxing champion who took to wrestling, this man was still in the ring in his late forties, carrying close to 300 pounds on his 6'6" frame. Name him.

8. Who was the University of Minnesota footballer who was also on the 1948 U.S. Olympic wrestling squad before turning professional and attaining the heavyweight championship in the late 1950s?

9. Who was the Oriental wrestler who preceded his matches with a ritual that included sprinkling salt in the four corners of the ring?

10. Who was the wrestler, born in Poland, who was a contemporary of Strangler Lewis and gave him highly competitive matches?

11. A failure as a wrestler while using the name Herman "Dutch" Rhode, who was the man who changed his name and used the description "Nature Boy" to find success?

12. Who was the black football star at UCLA who turned to pro wrestling before gaining stardom in Hollywood films?

42. Movies and Sports

What athletes were the subjects of these movies?

1. *Pride of the Yankees*
2. *Somebody Up There Likes Me*
3. *Fear Strikes Out*
4. *Pride of West Point*
5. *Monkey on My Back*
6. *The Pride of St. Louis*
7. *The Great White Hope*
8. *Brian's Song*

43. Magic Milers

Match these milers with the colleges they attended.

1. Glenn Cunningham
2. Tom O'Hara
3. Jim Beatty
4. Dyrol Burleson
5. Don Bowden
6. Bill Bonthron
7. Gil Dodds
8. Greg Rice
9. Les MacMitchell
10. Don Gehrmann

a) Princeton
b) New York University
c) Ashland
d) Wisconsin
e) North Carolina
f) Notre Dame
g) Loyola (Ill.)
h) California
i) Kansas
j) Oregon

44. Cool 3000

Which of these hitters failed to get 3000 hits in his major league career?

a) Paul Waner
b) Nap Lajoie
c) Rogers Hornsby

45. The Ladies Tee

1. The Ladies Professional Golfers Association was organized in 1948. Who was the first woman to win $100,000 under its auspices?

2. Who was the woman who won both the USGA Women's Open and LPGA championships in 1958 and again in 1961?

3. What amateur beat Susan Maxwell and Beth Stone to win the 1967 USGA Women's Open in 1967?

4. Who was the first American to win the British Ladies championship when she did it in 1947?

5. The first time the U.S. Women's Amateur tournament was held on the West Coast was in 1930, but it made no difference to whom as she won her fifth title?

6. Who was the woman from Uruguay who had won her country's national title twenty times before coming to the U.S. to win the Women's Open in 1955?

7. Marlene Bauer won the first Junior Girls Amateur championship in 1949. What was her married name when she was a leading money winner in the 1950s?

8. The first Curtis Cup matches were held in 1932 with the American women winning 5½ to 3½ over the British at Wentworth, England. Name the six members of the U.S. team.

9. What women's champion carded a record 62 for 18 holes on the 6286-yard long Hogan Park Course in Midland, Texas, in 1964?

10. Except for 1969, the LPGA's leading money-winner from 1965 through 1973 was Kathy Whitworth. Who led in 1969?

46. NBA Championships

1. The Boston Celtics won the first of their many championships in 1957 using nine men in the championship game. Who were they?

2. When Syracuse beat Fort Wayne, 92-91, in the final game of the 1955 championship series, it was the only time a seventh game had been decided by one point. Whose free throw made the difference?

3. Who holds the record for scoring the most points, 61, in a playoff game?

4. Only three times players have made 20 or more assists in playoff games. Earvin "Magic" Johnson did it twice. Who was the other?

4. Four men have had 19 assists in playoff games. Bob Cousy did it twice. Who were the others?

5. Minneapolis won the first NBA championship in 1950. Name the ten regulars on that Laker team.

6. Who holds the record for most personal fouls committed in a preliminary series game, set in the days of the Basketball Association of America?

7. The St. Louis Hawks in 1958, and the Philadelphia 76ers in 1967, interrupted Boston's championship string.

Name the regular members of the 1958 Hawks and 1967 76ers.

8. In a four-overtime playoff game in 1953, what Boston player scored 50 points, including 30 of 32 free throws?

47. Family Affair

1. Bruce Hale was basketball coach at Miami of Florida, and the star of his team married the coach's daughter. Who is the famous son-in-law?

2. Three Canadian brothers all played for the same hockey team at one time. Name them.

3. Who were the twins who were basketball stars at Seattle and a double play combination with the Pittsburgh Pirates?

4. One man led the American League in batting, and his brother was a leading rusher in the National Football League. Name them.

5. She was the first woman tennis pro to win $100,000 in competition, while her brother was a pitcher for the Giants. Who are they?

6. One man was a rookie defensive sensation in the NFL while a few years later his kid brother was a rookie star in the American Basketball Association. Name them.

7. Who were the look-alike twins who starred in basketball at Indiana but never played on the same team in the NBA?

8. The father was a basketball star at tiny Davis & Elkins College before he coached his son at Louisiana State. Name these basketball personalities.

9. What pair of over-sized brothers are the only twins ever named to the All-America football team?

10. Until Jim and Gaylord Perry broke the record, who were the pitchers with the record for most major league victories by two brothers (374)?

48. Where Did They Play?

Match these pro football stars with their colleges.

1. Sammy Baugh	a) Washington State
2. Lenny Moore	b) Wisconsin
3. Gino Marchetti	c) Columbia
4. Emlen Tunnell	d) Minnesota
5. Ken Strong	e) Marquette
6. Marion Motley	f) Indiana
7. Y. A. Tittle	g) Kentucky
8. Frank Kinard	h) Southern Methodist
9. Don Perkins	i) Stanford
10. Mel Hein	j) Oregon
11. Sid Luckman	k) Texas Christian
12. Johnny Sisk	l) West Virginia
13. George Blanda	m) Penn State
14. Ernie Nevers	n) New Mexico
15. Norm Van Brocklin	o) San Francisco
16. Joe Stydahar	p) Mississippi
17. Elroy Hirsch	q) Iowa
18. Leo Nomelleni	r) Louisiana State
19. Pete Pihos	s) New York University
20. Raymond Berry	t) Nevada

49. Stanley Cup Winners

1. In the 1955 final series, one team scored a record 27 goals to win the Cup. What two teams were involved and who was the winner?

2. In the 1932 playoffs, the winners took three straight games, scoring 6 goals in each game. Who were they and what team did they beat?

3. Detroit goalie Terry Sawchuk allowed just 5 goals in the eight games of the 1952 semi-final and final series. Against what two teams did he allow 0.62 goals a game?

4. Who was the goalie who was a two-time Stanley Cup MVP (Conn Smythe Trophy)?

5. In 1928, the winners of the final series scored only 5 goals. Who were they and whom did they beat?

6. It was the 1936 series, and a rookie who had scored only 2 goals in the regular season scored an overtime goal to give his team the victory, ending 2 hours, 56 minutes, and 30 seconds of scoreless hockey. Who was the player and his team?

7. Each team scored 9 goals in this seven-game series in 1945. Who won the cup?

8. Between 1956 and 1960, Montreal Canadiens won five straight Stanley Cups. Name the teams they beat at the beginning and end of the string.

9. In the 1942 series, Detroit won the first three games of the final series and then collapsed, losing four straight to whom?

10. In the 1965 final series, 136 penalties were called on what two teams? Who won the Cup?

50. Numbers Game

1. The record for largest crowd ever to see a single collegiate basketball game is 61,612. The date was March 29, 1982, and the setting the Louisiana Superdome. Who played in that NCAA championship game? (Note: Two days earlier the NCAA semifinal doubleheader drew the same number of spectators.)

2. On September 23, 1926, 120,757 gathered in Philadelphia's Sesquicentennial Stadium to see what two heavyweights in a championship fight?

3. The largest paid crowd for one tennis match was 30,492, gathered in Houston in 1973 to see whom?

4. The largest paid live crowd to see a basketball game was 75,000 in Berlin, Germany, to see whom?

5. The largest single game regular season crowd to see a National Football League game was 102,368 on November 10, 1957. Who played and where?

6. The largest crowd to see a boxing match, 135,132 in Milwaukee, August 18, 1941, saw what fight?

51. America's National Pastime

1. One home run gained what native of Glasgow, Scotland, who played with the Giants, a place in baseball history?

2. What 1966 World Series hero for Baltimore was born in Ozanna, Poland?

3. Pinch-hitting ability kept what native of Ribnik, Czechoslovakia, in the big leagues through 1961?

4. Who was the San Francisco Giant pitcher who was born in Otsuki, Japan?

5. Name the American League utility infielder of the 1950s and '60s who played with Detroit and Washington, and was born in St. Vito, Udine, Italy.

6. Who was the New York Met outfielder who learned to play baseball in Frederiksted, Virgin Islands?

7. What San Francisco and Chicago Cub infielder was born in Nassau, Bahamas?

8. Hawaii is not noted for its baseball players, but this Honolulu product once pinch-hit for Henry Aaron. Name him.

9. A native of Kos, Greece, he had a brief playing career as a second baseman, but stayed around a long time as a scout and front office executive with the Dodgers. Name him.

10. Who was the reserve catcher for the New York Yankees in the 1930s who was born in Modum, Norway?

11. "Pepper," as his St. Louis Brown teammates called this native of Swansea, Wales, ended his eighteen-year career in 1929. Name him.

52. Lending a Hand

Basketball is a team game, with sharp passing a requirement for championship teams. Name these top playmakers.

1. What center led the NBA with 702 assists in one season?

2. Who holds the NBA record of 29 assists in a single game?

3. Who holds the NBA record for highest assists-per-game average for one season?

4. Who holds the career assists record in the ABA?

5. The pivot play was devised by what center with the original Celtics?

6. Guards, naturally, dominate assist records, but what player who spent much of his career in the front court is among the top ten all-time assist leaders?

7. Who holds the single-season record for most assists in the ABA?

8. The ABA record for most assists in a game is 23. Who set it?

9. Who holds the record for assists by a rookie with 690?

10. What Rochester Royal was the first man to make 20 assists in a regular season NBA game?

53. Power-boat Racing

1. Who built *Miss America VIII* and set a world record of 75 miles per hour to win the Harmsworth Trophy in 1929?

2. Who was the man who won the President's Cup three straight years, 1950-52, and was killed in 1966 after winning the first two heats of a Gold Cup race?

3. The first boat to win the Harmsworth Cup three consecutive years was Canada's *Miss Supertest II*, 1959-61. Who owned it?

4. Who has won the Gold Cup more than any other man?

54. Slam

Which of these home run hitters did not hit at least 10 grand slams in his career?

    a) Mickey Mantle
    b) Gil Hodges
    c) Ernie Banks

55. Football Firsts

1. Who was the first Heisman Trophy winner?

2. The first college football game televised was in 1939, but when was the first network color telecast of a college game? Who played?

3. Who was the first black to play in the Sugar Bowl?

4. Who won the first American Football League championship game, January 1, 1961?

5. What was the result of the first College All-Star Game in 1934?

6. Who were the quarterback and receiver to complete football's first legal forward pass?

7. Which team coached by Wallace Wade was the first Southern school to play in the Rose Bowl?

8. Who was the first black quarterback in the NFL?

9. Easterners dominated the college All-America selections for more than a quarter of a century after Walter Camp began his selections. Who was the first player from a Pacific Coast school to make an All-America squad in 1921?

10. The Outland Trophy is awarded annually to the nation's best interior lineman. What Notre Dame tackle won the first Outland Trophy in 1946?

56. From "Over There"

In hockey, who is

1. The Chicago center born in Sokolce, Czechoslovakia, who first made the All-NHL team in 1961-62?

2. The native of Helsinki, Finland, who won the Calder Trophy when he broke in with the New York Rangers?

3. The all-league goalie born in Edinburgh, Scotland, who performed with the Black Hawks in the 1930s?

4. The lefty-shooting center who moved from Emsdetten, Germany, to South Porcupine, Ont., before joining the New York Rangers?

5. The goalie from Barry, Wales, who played with the Montreal Canadiens in the 1930s?

6. The left winger born in Odessa, Russia, who played eighteen seasons with the Chicago Black Hawks?

7. The proficient scorer born in Belfast, Ireland, who won the Calder Trophy in his rookie season with the Detroit Red Wings?

8. The man with a name made famous by Toronto natives but who himself came from Motherwell, Scotland, to be among the leading scorers with Detroit and Chicago after World War II?

9. The all-league defenseman for the New York Americans whose nickname was Cowboy even though he hailed from Edinburgh, Scotland?

57. Alias

Match the boxer on the left with his nickname on the right.

1. Archie Moore		a)	The Bronx Bull
2. Jack Dempsey		b)	Chalky
3. Jake LaMotta		c)	Boston Strongboy
4. Joe Louis		d)	Hammerin' Hank
5. Harry Greb		e)	Manassa Mauler
6. Primo Carnera		f)	The Orchid Man
7. Henry Armstrong		g)	The Mongoose
8. George Carpentier		h)	The Brown Bomber
9. John L. Sullivan		i)	The Ambling Alp
10. Albert Wright		j)	The Pittsburgh Windmill

58. Who Am I?

1. I was not especially known for my hitting, yet in the 1953 World Series I batted .500 and beat Babe Ruth's achievement of 22 total bases with two homers, two triples, a double, and seven singles. I also drove in eight runs. Who am I?

2. I played centerfield for nineteen years with the Washington Senators before going to Cleveland. During my career, which reached from 1915 to 1934, I had a lifetime batting average of .322 and was only 13 hits shy of the magic 3,000 circle, yet I didn't make the Hall of Fame until the special old-timers committee voted me in in 1963. Who am I?

3. I scattered only 5 hits in the fifth game of the 1956 World Series, yet the Yankees managed to get 2 runs while their pitcher, Don Larsen, was pitching a perfect game against my Dodgers. Who am I?

4. I played infield for twenty-five years, between 1906 and 1930, with the Chicago and Philadelphia teams in the American League. My lifetime batting average was .333, although the first hits came when I played under the name of Ed Sullivan. Who am I?

5. I pitched in the 1948 World Series, winning one game, saving another, and giving up no runs. I was the pitching star despite the presence of Bob Feller, Bob Lemon, Johnny Sain, and Warren Spahn. Who am I?

59. Making a Splash

1. Who was the first male swimmer to win the Sullivan Trophy, in 1964?

2. What Swede set thirty-one world records between 1921 and 1929?

3. Who was the only American man to receive a gold medal for swimming in the 1956 Olympics at Melbourne, when he won the 200-meter butterfly competition?

4. Who was the Indiana University swimmer who dominated breaststroke competition in the early 1960s, twice being named the outstanding performer in the National AAU championships?

5. Who was the breaststroke specialist known as "the Turk" who won the U.S. championship nine consecutive years?

6. Who were the Australian brother and sister who broke more than twenty world records in the late 1950s and early '60s?

7. A member of the Swimming Hall of Fame in Fort Lauderdale, this distance swimmer won five medals in the 1919 Inter-Allied Games and three gold medals in the 1920 Olympics. Name him.

8. What American, taking 26 hours and 50 minutes, became the first U.S. swimmer to cross the channel from England to France in 1923?

9. Who was the freestyle swimmer who won five national AAU titles in 1957 at distances from 400 to 1500 meters?

10. Who was the sprinting free-styler from Yale who was the first American to break 50 seconds indoors in the 100 meters, in 1944, and who broke the world record in that event seven times in all?

60. Mapping Basketball

1. Only two teams from east of the Hudson River have ever won the NCAA basketball title. Which are they?

2. What coach began recruiting New York City high school players to southern colleges via the "Underground Railway?"

3. Who was the "Wild West" shooter from Stanford who introduced the one-handed shot to the East?

4. Which school from west of the Mississippi River is the only one to have won the NIT twice, turning the trick in 1951 and again in 1966?

5. What teams from south of the Mason-Dixon Line other than Kentucky have won the NCAA championship?

61. Hockey Rookies

1. Who was the rookie goaltender who recorded 15 shutouts in a single season?

2. Who was the Detroit Red Wing who accounted for five assists in one game—a record for a rookie—against Chicago in 1947?

3. Who was the Montreal Maroon who scored 34 goals in thirty-six games during his rookie season in 1925-26?

4. Who is the Toronto rookie who took only fifteen seconds to score his first goal in his first NHL game in 1943?

5. Who was the first rookie with an expansion club to win the Calder Trophy?

6. Who is the man who beat out Chicago's Bobby Hull for rookie-of-the-year honors in the 1957-58 season?

7. Name the four rookies who have led the NHL in penalty minutes.

8. Name the six rookie goalies who won both the Calder Cup and a place on the first All-NHL team in the same year.

9. Gordie Howe is the all-time NHL scoring leader. What were his goal and assists totals in his rookie season of 1946-47?

10. Which Toronto Maple Leaf had been so badly wounded in World War II that he was told he would never play hockey again, yet won the Calder Trophy in 1947?

62. One of a Kind

1. Only one man in modern times has pitched a no-hitter in his first major league start. Name him.

2. Only one pitcher in the last 50 years has retired more than 27 consecutive batters in a single game. Who was he?

3. Only one batter has hit 18 home runs in a single calendar month. Who did it and in what month?

4. Who is the only man to complete an unassisted triple play in the World Series?

5. Who was the oldest man to win a major league batting title, when he hit .328 in 1958?

6. Who is the only rookie to have pitched a perfect game?

7. Who was the Pittsburgh Pirate who was the only man ever to hit more than 30 triples in one season when he hit thirty-six in 1912?

8. Though he was good enough to spend more than 20 years in the majors, this hurler has the dubious distinction of being the only pitcher to throw four wild pitches in one inning. Name him.

9. Since rookie-of-the-year awards were instituted in 1947 only one shortstop has been so honored in the National League. Who was he?

10. Only one non-pitcher in the Hall of Fame has a lifetime batting average of less than .255. A catcher, he played between 1912 and 1929, primarily with the White Sox. Name him.

63. Pigskin Thieves

1. What former Redskin and Viking defender holds the NFL record with 81 interceptions in his career?

2. Though he became a coach whose college teams were noted for an explosive offense, this man was among the leading pass interceptors as a collegian at Oklahoma from 1946 to 1949.

3. Two players have intercepted passes and returned them 102 yards for touchdowns in the NFL. The first was Detroit's Bob Smith in 1949. What New York Giant matched this feat in 1961?

4. While playing for Michigan State in the late 1940s, this defender returned 20 interceptions for 410 yards to establish a national career record. Name him.

5. Though he spent most of his NFL days in Chicago and Detroit, this defensive back was with the Rams when he picked off a record 14 passes in 1952. Name him.

6. Who was the college defenseman of the early 1950s who averaged 32.9 yards a return with 10 interceptions in his college career at Colgate?

7. A dozen or more players have intercepted 4 passes in a single NFL game, but this two-way player for the Washington Redskins was the first to do it (in 1943). Who was he?

8. From 1950 to 1952, this Illinois defensive halfback intercepted 29 passes and had a string of fifteen straight games in which he intercepted a pass. Name him.

9. In 1972, Oakland's Jack Tatum traveled 104 yards with a recovered fumble. Whose record did he break?

10. Though drafted as a quarterback as an NFL bonus pick, this player led the nation in pass interceptions as an Oregon freshman in 1951. Name him.

64. Trophy

Match the schools in the outside columns with the trophy in the center column that their football teams have played for.

A) Michigan	1. Old Oaken Bucket	a) Northwestern
B) Notre Dame	2. Old Shoe	b) Purdue
C) Illinois	3. The Teacup	c) Missouri
D) New Mexico	4. Beanpot	d) Bucknell
E) California	5. Little Brown Jug	e) Southern California
F) Clemson	6. Osage War Drum	f) Boston University
G) Syracuse	7. The Shillelagh	g) Arizona
H) Indiana	8. The Axe	h) Minnesota
I) Kansas	9. The Tomahawk	i) Stanford
J) Temple	10. Kit Carson Rifle	j) South Carolina

65. For Openers

1. Only one pitcher has thrown a no-hitter on the opening day of the baseball season. Name him.

2. What team has opened at home more than any other?

3. On opening day of 1946, one of the all-time leading home run hitters slammed the last homer of his career. Name him.

4. Who is the current major league manager who helped win an opening-day game for the Milwaukee Braves in 1955 by hitting a pinch-hit home run in his first time at bat in the major leagues?

5. Who christened Yankee Stadium's first opening-day game with a three-run homer in 1923?

6. One of the best opening-day pitching records belongs to what Hall of Fame pitcher who won nine of fourteen season starters?

66. Grand Total

Which of these runners never had a 1000-yard rushing season in the NFL?

   a) Rick Casares
   b) Paul Hornung
   c) Dick Bass

67. NFL History

1. Which NFL team first drafted John Unitas?

2. What NFL team began life as the Frankford Yellow Jackets?

3. The first playoff game between divisional leaders came in 1933. Who beat whom?

4. What NFL team was once sponsored by the Staley Starch Company?

5. What teams share the distinction of losing more NFL playoff games (15) than any other?

6. When was the last time that a team failed to throw a forward pass in a regular season game?

7. What pre-Super Bowl era NFL championship game was decided indoors?

8. The first million-dollar gate for an NFL championship game came in 1961. Who beat whom, and where?

9. Who were the two players suspended in 1964 for betting on their own teams?

10. Who made the winning score in the NFL's first sudden-death overtime game in 1958?

68. NBA All-Stars

1. Which of these players never made the first All-NBA team?

        a) Richie Guerin
        b) Jack Twyman
        c) Carl Braun
        d) Tom Heinsohn
        e) Hal Greer
        f) Sam Jones
        g) Cliff Hagan
        h) Bobby Wanzer
        i) Slater Martin
        j) Gus Johnson

2. Four players made the first All-NBA team three consecutive years, 1962-64. Name them.

3. What Philadelphia 76er scored 19 points in one quarter of the 1968 All-Star Game, earning MVP honors for his efforts?

4. Only two men have averaged 20 points a game in their more than ten All-Star Games appearances. Who are they?

5. What two men are the only ones to have fouled out of two All-Star Games each?

6. Eleven men have played in the All-Star Game and then returned to coach one of the All-Star teams. How many can you name?

7. The most points scored by one player in an All-Star Game is 42 in 1962. Who scored them?

8. Also in the 1962 game, one man pulled down a record 27 rebounds. Name him.

9. Who attempted a record 27 field goals in the 1967 All-Star Game and made 16 of them?

10. Rookie All-Stars are rare, but which one made 14 assists—a record at the time—in the 1961 All-Star Game?

69. Fielding Pitchers

1. Name the San Diego pitcher who handled more chances in a single season, 112, than any other pitcher without making an error.

2. What Philadelphia Athletic pitcher holds the record of 7 putouts in one game, set in 1949?

3. What Chicago Cub pitcher handled 273 consecutive chances between 1941 and 1946 without committing an error?

4. Only one National League pitcher has ever recorded three putouts in one inning when he accomplished the feat with the Cubs in 1965. Name him.

5. What New York Giant pitcher holds the career record of 40 chances handled in World Series competition?

6. Two American League pitchers have participated in four double plays in one game. What White Sox pitcher did it in 1932, and what Tiger duplicated the feat in 1948?

7. What Cleveland pitcher led the American League pitchers in fielding six times between 1948 and 1956?

8. What Yankee pitcher holds the career record of 11 putouts in World Series competition?

9. Four pitchers have participated in two double plays in a single World Series game. Chief Bender did it in 1914 and L.A. Bush in 1922. Name the Yankee in 1951 and the Royal in 1980 who duplicated the achievement.

10. What Minnesota pitcher had a record 5 putouts in one World Series game in 1965?

70. Fielding Catchers

1. What Detroit catcher holds the major league record with a fielding percentage of .9932?

2. What National League catcher had a record 20 putouts in a game in 1970?

3. Who is the catcher, playing for Cleveland and the Philadelphia Athletics in 1945, who had a hand in a record 29 double plays?

4. What American League catcher holds the record of handling 950 consecutive chances without committing an error?

5. What post-1900 player set the record of 1,810 assists as a catcher while playing with the White Sox?

6. What Dodger catcher had a record 18 putouts in one 1963 World Series game?

7. What National Leaguer holds the record with 67 putouts in one World Series, set in 1973?

8. What Houston catcher set a National League record by playing in 138 consecutive games without making an error?

9. What New York Giant catcher holds the record of four passed balls in one inning, set in 1954?

10. Since 1950, only one National League catcher has participated in as many as three double plays in a single game. Name the Brave who accomplished this.

71. Fielding First Basemen

1. The last unassisted triple play by a first baseman was performed in 1927. What Detroit Tiger accomplished this feat?

2. Before Steve Garvey came along, what Dodger first baseman held the record for best career fielding average at the position?

3. What Philadelphia Athletic first baseman participated in a record 194 double plays in 1949?

4. Who was the Boston Brave first baseman who handled a record 43 chances in the 26-inning game of May 1, 1920?

5. What first baseman holds the record of 326 career putouts in the World Series?

6. Two St. Louis first basemen, one Cardinal and one Brown, each completed eight unassisted double plays in a season. Name them.

7. Four first basemen—two in each league—have committed three errors in one inning. Name them.

8. What Pirate first baseman holds the record with eight assists in one game, set back in 1971?

9. What traveling first baseman who came into the majors in 1968 holds the American League record with a career field percentage of .9949 while playing for five different clubs?

10. Known for his mistakes, this first baseman holds the career record for World Series errors at his position, making eight between 1911 and 1918. Name him.

72. Fielding Second Basemen

1. Who led the National League in fielding percentage seven times, more than anyone else?

2. What California Angel infielder, playing in 1966, set the modern record of 12 putouts by a second baseman in one game?

3. In 1964 and 1965, who set the American League standard by handling 458 consecutive chances without committing an error?

4. Who appeared in more World Series games as a second baseman than any other player?

5. A Cleveland second baseman completed the only triple play in World Series history when he performed unassisted in the 1920 World Series. Name him.

6. Two Brooklyn second basemen were the first two players in history to make 12 assists in a game. John Ward did it in 1892, who duplicated the feat in 1956?

7. Who holds the American League mark for the best one-season fielding percentage by a second baseman?

8. What Hall of Fame second baseman committed 5 errors in a single game in 1915?

9. What Chicago Cub handled a then-record 418 chances between June 13 and September 5, 1962, without making an error?

10. Two second basemen have participated in 150 or more double plays in one season. What Tiger was in 150 in 1950 and what Pirate set the record of 161 in 1961?

73. Fielding Third Basemen

1. What Washington Senator played in a record 576 consecutive games at third base?

2. Since 1930, only one third baseman has had seven put-outs in one game. What Detroit Tiger accomplished this in 1954?

3. Brooks Robinson holds the major league record for assists by a third baseman. Who holds the National League career record?

4. What former National Leaguer moved to the AL and in 1974 set a record with a .9894 fielding percentage at third base?

5. What Giant third baseman holds the major league record of playing in 97 consecutive games without committing an error?

6. What Detroit third baseman had a record 30 assists in the 1940 World Series against Cincinnati?

7. Playing with the Athletics and Yankees between 1910 and 1921, who established the record of 37 putouts by a third baseman in the World Series?

8. Five third basemen have been named Rookie of the Year since the award was instituted in 1947. Name the two American Leaguers and three in the senior circuit who made it.

9. Five National League third basemen since 1960 have committed three errors in a single inning. Name them.

10. What Pittsburgh Hall of Fame third baseman led the National League in errors five times during his eighteen-year career?

74. Fielding Shortstops

1. Who was the last shortstop to complete an unassisted triple play?

2. Only one American League shortstop has participated in six double plays in one game. Name this Oakland A.

3. What shortstop has appeared in more World Series games than any other?

4. What Hall of Fame shortstop holds the major league record of 5,133 putouts in a career?

5. Only one shortstop had 3 putouts in one inning in a World Series game. It happened in 1968. Name this Detroit Tiger.

6. What Washington Senator committed a record 8 errors in the 1925 World Series against the Pirates?

7. Who held the American League career fielding record before Mark Belanger completed his career at shortstop with a .9768 mark for Baltimore?

8. What Montreal Expo participated in 137 double plays in 1970?

9. Who was the New York Giant shortstop who handled 383 consecutive chances without committing an error between July 28, 1946, and May 25, 1947?

10. What American Leaguer played more games at shortstop than any other major league player?

75. Fielding in the Corn

1. Who holds the best career fielding average for an outfielder?

2. Who is the outfielder who played in a record 266 consecutive games with the Phillies and Tigers in the early 1960s without committing an error?

3. What Boston Red Sox outfielder set the league record for a 154-game season with 503 putouts in 1948?

4. Who holds the career record of 450 assists by an outfielder?

5. The record for most chances by an outfielder in a modern World Series was set by what Cub in 1945?

6. Who committed more errors (271) than any other outfielder during his twenty-four seasons with Detroit and the Philadelphia Athletics?

7. What Chicago "Black Sox" outfielder set a record by participating in 15 double plays during the 1919 season?

8. What St. Louis Cardinal handled 568 chances without committing an error between September 3, 1965, and June 4, 1967?

9. What Cleveland Indian, in 1968, was the last outfielder to complete two unassisted double plays in one season?

10. What Dodger set the single inning and single game records by making 3 errors in the fifth inning of the second game of the 1966 World Series?

76. Friendly Competitors

It is rare that two men from the same college backfield shared national attention, but it happened with these players. Match the players and their colleges.

a) Clendon Thomas
b) Curtis McLinton
c) Floyd Little
d) Doak Walker
e) Pervis Atkins
f) Charley Flowers
g) Bob Anderson
h) Hugh McElhanney
i) Larry Dupree
j) Don Clark
k) Abe Woodson

1. Southern Methodist
2. Illinois
3. New Mexico State
4. Ohio State
5. Army
6. Washington
7. Kansas
8. Mississippi
9. Oklahoma
10. Syracuse
11. Florida

A) Pete Dawkins
B) Don Heinrich
C) Jake Gibbs
D) Larry Csonka
E) Steve Spurrier
F) Tommy McDonald
G) Bob White
H) J. C. Caroline
I) Bob Gaiters
J) Kyle Rote
K) Bert Coan

77. Goose Eggs

Which of these pitchers never had a no-hitter?
   a) Walter Johnson
   b) Lefty Grove
   c) Bob Lemon

78. Mermaids

1. Who was the first woman to swim across the English Channel?

2. Who was the sixteen-year-old California girl who won five national AAU swimming titles in 1968?

3. Four of the five women who received the Sullivan Award as America's outstanding amateur athlete were swimmers or divers. Name the 1944, 1956, 1968, and 1978 winners.

4. A grand total of forty-three world records was set by what Danish woman between 1936 and 1942?

5. Honored as Woman Athlete of the Year in 1931, who was the swimmer who won two gold medals for the U.S. in the 1932 Olympics?

6. In 1951, who became the first woman to swim the English Channel in both directions?

7. What twelve-year-old American girl won an Olympic gold medal for springboard diving in 1920?

8. The U.S. women at the 1960 Olympics were called the "water babies" because of their youth. Who was their sixteen-year-old leader who captured three gold medals and a silver?

9. Who was the versatile woman who won twenty-four swimming titles and five diving titles in the 1930s?

10. Pat McCormick won four Olympic gold medals for diving in the 1950s, but only one American woman won one for swimming—this in the 100-meter butterfly event in 1956. Who was she?

79. Part of a Whole

Some professional basketball players had nicknames that seemed to be part of their whole name, a three-part name that rolls out as readily as William Jennings Bryan. Well, let's see. Fill in the blanks.

1. William _____ Kennedy
2. Alex _____ Ellis
3. Charles _____ Vaughn
4. Goebel _____ Ritter
5. Harry _____ Jeannette
6. Duane _____ Thoren
7. Leo _____ Klier
8. Jim _____ Ligon
9. John _____ Dillon
10. Bob _____ Nordmann
11. Jack _____ Garfinkel
12. Lloyd _____ Dove
13. John _____ Reiser
14. Charles _____ Nash
15. Ted _____ McLain

80. Women in Tennis

1. Who was the American woman who won the singles, doubles, and mixed doubles titles in both the Wimbledon and the U.S. Nationals in 1939?

2. Name the American woman who won the Wimbledon title eight times and the U.S. singles championship seven times before retiring in 1938.

3. What American was the first woman ever to hold the Wimbledon, French, Australian, and American singles titles simultaneously?

4. Who was the Australian who became the second woman to complete the Grand Slam in 1970?

5. Who is the American woman who won her first Wimbledon title in 1914 and her nineteenth in 1934, all in women's doubles and mixed doubles?

6. In 1967 at Wimbledon, Maria Bueno and Nancy Richey lost a doubles match that took a record thirty-eight games to decide. Who beat them?

7. What woman was the first black to play in the U.S. Nationals at Forest Hills in 1950?

8. Who was the woman who created a sensation by wearing lace panties on the court?

9. Who were the doubles partners who won the U.S. Women's championship nine consecutive years, 1942-50?

10. Who was "the first lady of American tennis"?

81. The Minors

Several cities had minor league baseball teams with very distinctive nicknames. Match these cities and appellations.

1. Toledo	a)	Millers
2. Montreal	b)	Dukes
3. Louisville	c)	Seals
4. Rochester	d)	Marlins
5. Minneapolis	e)	Crackers
6. San Francisco	f)	Jets
7. Albuquerque	g)	Royals
8. Miami	h)	Red Wings
9. Columbus	i)	Mud Hens
10. Atlanta	j)	Sluggers

82. NIT Tidbits

1. What major league baseball player was the National Invitational Tourament's Most Valuable Player while playing basketball for Ohio University in 1941?

2. St. Bonaventure scored a record 354 points in the 1960 tournament but didn't make the finals. Who did?

3. Kentucky beat Rhode Island, 46-45, to win the 1946 NIT. Whose free throw made the difference?

4. Which was the first small college to win the NIT?

5. NCAA champion Kentucky lost two games in the 1948-49 season, one of them in the quarter-finals of the NIT. Who beat the Wildcats?

6. Dayton was runner-up five times before winning an NIT in 1962. Who did Dayton beat and what Flyer was MVP?

7. What All-American football player scored 10 points in a losing effort as Temple beat Colorado, 60-36, in the first NIT?

8. Bradley hit 62 percent of its shots to win the 1964 NIT. What Rocky Mountain school was the victim of this hot shooting?

9. Who were the Brigham Young stars who led the Cougars to the 1951 championship?

10. What team was the first to win two NIT crowns?

11. Kentucky, with Ralph Beard, Wah Wah Jones, and Alex Groza, failed to win the NIT in 1947. Who did?

12. The 1939 NIT title game featured two undefeated teams, Loyola (Chicago) and Long Island University. Who won?

13. In 1945, the tourney MVP scored 120 points in three games, including 53 points in one contest. Who was this 6′ 10″ center and what team did he play for?

14. "Easy Ed" Macauley outplayed Dolph Schayes in the 1948 NIT championship game, leading what team to the title?

83. In Their Cups

Periodic or annual awards and trophies have long played a part in sport, often marking the highlight of a year or bringing special attention to an individual or team. Who plays for or receives

1. The Heisman Trophy
2. The Art Ross Trophy
3. The Podoloff Award
4. The Sullivan Award
5. The Wightman Cup
6. The Curtis Cup
7. The Davis Cup
8. The Ryder Cup
9. The Cy Young Award
10. Eisenhower Trophy
11. Grey Cup
12. Stanley Cup
13. Walker Cup
14. MacArthur Bowl
15. Edward J. McNeil Award
16. Colonial Cup
17. Maxwell Trophy
18. Naismith Trophy

84. Feats of Air

1. Of the top twenty passers in the history of the NFL, which one has the best average of yards gained per pass?

2. In 1964, this Tulsa University quarterback threw 7 touchdown passes in a single game. Name him.

3. Only two men have caught passes for more than 300 yards in a single NFL game. A Cleveland player did it in 1945, while a Detroit Lion achieved this total in 1950. Name them.

4. Who was the University of Texas-El Paso quarterback who threw 943 passes in his varsity career from 1965 to 1967?

5. Only two pro receivers have ever caught passes for more than 1500 yards in a single season. Lance Alworth did it once. Which other AFL player turned the trick twice?

6. Who was the University of Cincinnati quarterback who threw for a record 554 yards in a game against Ohio University?

7. Which professional quarterback was intercepted more times in his career than any other?

8. Though better known as a defensive halfback, this man was on the receiving end of a 98-yard scoring pass from Ogden Compton for the Chicago Cardinals in 1955. Name him.

9. This Southern Methodist quarterback led the nation in passing percentage in 1957, connection on 71 of 102 attempts. Name him.

10. There have been four 99-yard touchdown passes thrown in the NFL. Match the quarterbacks and receivers who completed the play.

1. Frank Filchock	a) Pat Studstill
2. George Izo	b) Gerry Allen
3. Karl Sweetan	c) Andy Farkas
4. Sonny Jurgenson	d) Bobby Mitchell

85. Auto Racing

1. Who has won the Daytona 500 more than any other driver?

2. A victory in 1961 brought whom the distinction of being the first three-time winner of the Sebring Grand Prix of Endurance?

3. Who is the only one to win the United States Grand Prix three consecutive years (1963-65)?

4. The first running of the Daytona 500 in 1959 required a photo finish to determine the winner. Who was it, Lee Petty or Johnny Beauchamp?

5. Who is "The Flying Texan" who is one of the rare three-time winners of the Indianapolis 500?

86. Nom de Ring

Match the men on the left with the boxing names they used, on the right.

1. Walker Smith
2. Sidney Walker
3. Barnet Rasofsky
4. Joseph Berardinelli
5. William Papaleo
6. Gerardo Gonzalez
7. Rocco Barbella
8. Barney Lebrowitz
9. Arnold Cream
10. Joseph Youngs

a) Tommy Ryan
b) Rocky Graziano
c) Jersey Joe Walcott
d) Kid Gavilan
e) Battling Levinsky
f) Barney Ross
g) Sugar Ray Robinson
h) Joey Maxim
i) Beau Jack
j) Willie Pep

87. Blank-Blank

Only one of these pitchers hurled a no-hitter. Which one?

a) Grover Alexander
b) Dizzy Dean
c) Carl Hubbell

88. Baseball Majors

Match the major league players with the colleges they attended.

1.	Wally Moon	a)	Minnesota
2.	Robin Roberts	b)	Duke
3.	Lou Gehrig	c)	Oklahoma State
4.	Lou Boudreau	d)	Wisconsin
5.	Dick Groat	e)	Louisiana State
6.	Harvey Kuenn	f)	Missouri
7.	Steve Hamilton	g)	Indiana
8.	Bill Skowron	h)	Illinois
9.	Bob Gibson	i)	Mississippi State
10.	Jerry Kindall	j)	Columbia
11.	Jerry Adair	k)	Creighton
12.	Alvin Dark	l)	Michigan State
13.	Ted Klusewski	m)	Purdue
14.	Don Kessinger	n)	Texas A&M
15.	Sonny Seibert	o)	Morehead State

89. Receiving Ends

There have been many notable passing combinations in both professional football and in the college ranks. Some brought their teams championships, others were record-setters. Some of the combinations were memorable for just a season or even a single game. Match them.

1. Steve Tensi	a) Ken Kavanaugh
2. Y. A. Tittle	b) Buddy Dial
3. Otto Graham	c) Pat Richter
4. Jerry Rhome	d) Fred Biletnikoff
5. Jim Plunkett	e) Chris Burford
6. Ron Vander Kelen	f) Knute Rockne
7. John Unitas	g) Del Shofner
8. Bob Waterfield	h) Dante Lavelli
9. Cecil Isbell	i) Elroy Hirsch
10. Sid Luckman	j) Howard Twilley
11. King Hill	k) Raymond Berry
12. Dick Norman	l) Randy Vataha
13. Gus Dorais	m) Don Hutson

90. World Series Pinch-hitting

1. Who was the Yankee catcher who set a World Series record for most plate appearances in a career as a pinch-hitter when he came to bat ten times in the 1960s?

2. When the Dodgers were in the Series against the White Sox in 1959, this man pinch-hit four times and got 2 hits, both of them home runs. Name him.

3. This New York player appeared in only 576 regular season games in his entire career, but in the World Series of 1954 he was the batting star as a pinch-hitter. Name him.

4. When St. Louis was winning the Series in 1942 and again in 1944, this Cardinal had three pinch-hits in each series. Name him.

5. It was the Braves vs. the Yankees in 1957, and this Milwaukee pinch-batter claimed he was hit with a pitched ball and even produced a ball with shoe polish on it to prove his point. Name him.

6. Whose pinch-hit in the 1947 Dodger-Yankee Series broke up Bill Bevens' no-hit bid?

91. College Strongmen

Match these shotputters and discus throwers with the colleges they attended.

1. Harold Connolly	**a)** Utah
2. Al Oerter	**b)** New York University
3. Parry O'Brien	**c)** Emporia (Kan.)
4. Randy Matson	**d)** Yale
5. Gary Gubner	**e)** Boston College
6. Jack Torrance	**f)** Manhattan
7. Ken Bantum	**g)** Southern California
8. Al Feurbach	**h)** Kansas
9. Fortune Gordien	**i)** Texas A&M
10. Jim Fuchs	**j)** Louisiana State
11. Jay Silvester	**k)** Minnesota

92. Hockey Matches

Hook up the nickname in the left column with the man in the right.

1. Turk		a)	Fred Patrick
2. King		b)	George Boucher
3. Bun		c)	Irvine Bailey
4. Toe		d)	Clarence Abel
5. Rocket		e)	Bernie Geoffrion
6. Pocket Rocket		f)	Walter Broda
7. Boom-Boom		g)	Maurice Richard
8. Muzz		h)	Henri Richard
9. Taffy		i)	Frederick Cook
10. Bep		j)	Charles McVeigh
11. Ace		k)	Ralph Weiland
12. Ching		l)	J. Armand Guidlin
13. Buck		m)	Francis Michael Clancy
14. Rabbit		n)	Hector Blake
15. Cooney		o)	Ivan Johnson

93. Portsiders

Almost all left-handed pitchers or batters are dubbed "Lefty," and for many the nickname sticks. Identify these lefties:

1. Before Denny McLain turned the trick in 1968, this Lefty was the last American League pitcher to win 30 games in a season.

2. This hard-hitting Lefty with Philadelphia set the National League record for most hits in a season with 254 back in 1929.

3. One of the many New York Yankees of the 1930s to make the Hall of Fame, this Lefty's best season was 1934, when he compiled a 26-5 won-lost record.

4. In twelve years with the Braves and Cubs between 1910 and 1921 this Lefty struck out 1003 batters and hurled 31 shutouts.

5. This Lefty was a top-notch pitcher with Chicago, completing back-to-back 20-game winning seasons before being implicated in the 1919 World Series scandal.

94. Starting Small

Many professional basketball stars came from smaller institutions. Match the players and their colleges.

1. Gus Johnson	a) Iona
2. Harry Gallatin	b) Morris Harvey
3. Nat Clifton	c) West Virginia State
4. Woody Sauldsberry	d) Northeast Missouri
5. George King	e) Idaho
6. Vern Mikklesen	f) Xavier (La.)
7. Sam Jones	g) North Carolina College
8. Richie Guerin	h) Louisiana Tech
9. Earl Lloyd	i) Texas Southern
10. Jackie Moreland	j) Hamline

95. Army and Navy

1. Who was Army's "lonesome end" in the Cadets' 22-6 football victory over Navy in 1958?

2. What Navy Heisman Trophy winner turned down a $60,000 offer to play baseball?

3. Who scored the three touchdowns in Army's 23-7 victory over Navy in 1944?

4. Playing in Chicago in 1926, Lighthorse Harry Wilson gave Army a commanding lead. Whose dropkicks gave Navy a 21-21 tie?

5. Unbeaten and untied Army was shot down by Navy, 14-2, in the 1950 game. Who did the Middie passing?

6. Name the backfield that helped Heisman Trophy-winner Roger Staubach to national honors in the early 1960s.

7. Who was Army's Coach of the Year in 1966 when he guided the Cadets to an 8-2 record and victory over Navy?

8. What Navy All-America halfback ran Army ragged in the mud in the Middies' 1934 victory?

9. In 1945, the middle of the Doc Blanchard and Glenn Davis era, Army had six All-Americans on the team. Name them.

10. Navy failed to win a game in 1948, but managed to tie Army, 21-21. Who were the Middie heroes?

96. Antwerp Olympics

1. A pole vault of 13′5″ was a world and Olympic record in 1920. What American set it?

2. What thirty-six-year-old Briton scored a double in the 800- and 1500-meter runs?

3. What Hawaiian, representing the U.S., won the gold medal in the 100-meter freestyle swim?

4. What U.S. woman swimmer not only won the 100-meter freestyle, but also the 300-meter event, the only time this competition was held?

5. Who was the twelve-year-old American girl who won a gold medal in springboard diving?

97. Paris Olympics

1. Paavo Nurmi won what three events at Paris in 1924?

2. Who was Nurmi's Finnish teammate who won the 10,000 meters and the steeplechase?

3. Tennis was an Olympic sport in 1924, and what U.S. women's winner was known as "Little Miss Poker Face"?

4. Who was the American swimming star who won the 100- and 400-meter events and anchored the 800-meter relay team?

5. What U.S. woman swimmer won the first of two straight gold medals in the 400-meter freestyle?

98. Amsterdam Olympics

1. In 1928, women's track and field events were scheduled for the first time. Who was the only American to win a gold medal (in the 100 meters) ?

2. What American scored a double, winning both the men's springboard and platform diving?

3. Who was the Canadian teenager who won both the men's 100- and 200-meter dashes?

4. What football player teamed with George Baird, Fred Alderman, and Bud Spence to set a world record of 3:14.2 in the 1600-meter relay?

5. The Finns dominated the distance events, but an Algerian representing France won the marathon. Who was it?

99. Los Angeles Olympics (1932)

1. What Italian upset Glenn Cunningham in the 1,500-meter run at the Coliseum in 1932?

2. Babe Didrikson won gold medals in what two events?

3. What swimmer "trained on champagne" to win the 100-meter backstroke?

4. What American man won both the 100- and the 200-meter dashes?

5. Japanese men dominated the swimming events, but one American won a gold medal in the 400-meter freestyle. Name him.

100. Berlin Olympics

1. In what four events did Jesse Owens win his four gold medals in 1936?

2. Glenn Cunningham again failed to win the 1,500 meters. Who beat him this time?

3. Dorothy Poynton won the platform diving competition in 1932 and repeated that triumph in Berlin under her married name. What was it?

4. The first U.S. gold medal winner was a black man snubbed by Hitler in the victory ceremony. Who was the man and what was the event?

5. What crew of collegians won the fifth straight eight-oar rowing title for the United States?

101. London Olympics

1. Harrison Dillard was regarded as the best hurdler in the world in 1948, yet he didn't make the U.S. team in that event. In what did he win his gold medal?

2. What Dutch woman, called "Fabulous Fanny" won both dashes and the 80-meter hurdles?

3. Who was the Czech "Iron Man" who won the 10,000 meters?

4. This American won the first of two platform diving medals in 1948. Name him.

5. What Americans were the first two finishers in the 200-meter dash?

102. Helsinki Olympics

1. What American with a famous baseball name won the javelin competition in 1956?

2. Who were the members of the Jamaican 1600-meter relay team that won the gold medal with a record time of 3:03.9?

3. Who was the U.S. woman who won the first two of her four gold medals for diving?

4. The winner of the 800-meter run was timed in 1:49.2; the same time that had earned him Olympic gold in London. Name him.

5. It happened in Helsinki; an American finally won the steeplechase. Who was he?

103. Melbourne Olympics

1. In 1956, this Australian woman won the first of three consecutive 100-meter freestyle titles. Name her.

2. In the United States he had represented Villanova, but in the Olympics, he won the metric mile for Ireland. What was his name?

3. The United States had two weight-lifting champions at Melbourne. Name them.

4. Who was the Texan who captured both men's sprints?

5. Who was the Australian swimming star who won both the 400- and the 1500-meter freestyle events in world record time?

104. Rome Olympics

1. Who was the barefoot Ethiopian who won the marathon in 1960?

2. Ray Norton and Dave Sime represented the U.S., but they failed to win either sprint. Who did?

3. What American woman won three gold medals in track and field?

4. This California blonde lowered the 400-meter free-style record to 4:50.6. Name her.

5. The Olympic high-jump record finally moved above 7 feet, but neither John Thomas nor Valery Brumel won the gold medal. Who did?

105. Tokyo Olympics

1. The women's 400-meter individual medley was a swimming event introduced in 1964. What American won it?

2. The U.S. won the 5000- and 10,000-meter runs for the first time. Who did it?

3. As it had in every previous Olympic games, America won the pole vault at Tokyo. What Rice Institute dental student took the gold?

4. Who was the German who broke the thirty-two-year hold the U.S. had on the decathlon?

5. Who anchored the U.S. 400-meter relay team behind Paul Drayton, Gerry Ashworth, and Dick Stebbins?

106. Mexico City Olympics

1. What American swimmer in 1968 was the first woman to win three gold medals in individual events?

2. Who was the weightman who won a gold medal for the fourth consecutive Olympics?

3. The 1600-meter relay record was lowered to 2:56.1. What four U.S. runners did it?

4. Who broke the long-jump record by nearly three feet with a leap of 29'2¼"?

5. What U.S. woman won the 800-meter run in Olympic record time of 2:00.9?

107. Munich Olympics

1. The pole vault record moved above 18 feet in 1972, but for the first time in history an American failed to win the event. Who did?

2. What American was the upset winner of the marathon?

3. Who was the Russian who won both the men's 100- and 200-meter dashes?

4. What were the two individual events in which Olga Korbut of the U.S.S.R. won gold medals?

5. Australia's Shane Gould won three gold medals in swimming. What member of the U.S. women's team also won three gold medals in swimming?

108. Winners

Which of these professional teams is the only one to have won a league championship?

    a) Patriots
    b) Falcons
    c) Bills

109. Court Connection

Match these NBA players with their nicknames.

1.	Tom Sanders	a)	Bad News
2.	Frank Saul	b)	Monk
3.	Wallace Jones	c)	Satch
4.	John Abramovic	d)	Sweetwater
5.	John Havlicek	e)	Wah Wah
6.	Don Meineke	f)	Happy
7.	Andrew Levane	g)	Pep
8.	Nat Clifton	h)	Bones
9.	Horace McKinney	i)	Brooms
10.	Wade Halbrook	j)	Fuzzy
11.	Jim Barnes	k)	Hondo
12.	Harold Hairston	l)	Swede

110. Hey, Rube!

Many baseball players have carried the nickname "Rube." Identify these.

1. Christened Richard, this Rube's career extended from 1908 to 1925. One of his best seasons was 1912, when he won 19 straight games for the New York Giants.

2. This Rube was a catcher starting out with the Chicago Cubs before moving to Brooklyn, where he was used as a pinch-hitter and back-up man for Roy Campanella.

3. When Babe Ruth hit his 60 home runs, he hit only 19 off left-handed pitchers. Who was Philadelphia's southpaw Rube who served up 4 home runs to the Babe?

4. This Hall of Fame Rube struck out 343 batters in 1904 while pitching for Connie Mack's Athletics. He also hurled 5 shutouts in his fourteen-year career.

5. This Rube pitched for Cincinnati and the New York Giants between 1910 and 1925. With the Giants in the 1917 World Series, he didn't allow an earned run in 15⅔ innings.

6. An outstanding pitcher with such turn-of-the-century teams as the Cuban X Giants and Negro teams in Michigan and Texas, this Rube was one of the founders of the National Negro League, which flourished in the 1920s.

7. A left-handed pitcher, this Rube pitched two complete game victories for the World Series-winning Boston Red Sox in 1915.

111. What's in a Name?

Some NFL players have been more readily identified by their nicknames than by their given names. Supply the real names of

1. Red Grange		a)	Orban
2. Dutch Clark		b)	Verda
3. Bulldog Turner		c)	Clarence
4. Sonny Randle		d)	Fred
5. Buddy Young		e)	Paul
6. Link Lyman		f)	Wilbur
7. Bruiser Kinard		g)	Gilbert
8. Dub Jones		h)	Harold
9. Spec Sanders		i)	Roy
10. Ace Parker		j)	Vito
11. Tank Younger		k)	Earl
12. Buddy Dial		l)	Walter
13. Babe Parilli		m)	Claude
14. Bud McFaddin		n)	Harry
15. Vitamin Smith		o)	Earl
16. Fuzzy Thurston		p)	William
17. Fats Henry		q)	Lewis
18. Jug Girard		r)	Frank
19. Waddy Young		s)	Ulmo
20. Chick Jagade		t)	Clyde

112. The Scorers

1. After seven straight years as NBA scoring king, Wilt Chamberlain was deposed by whom in 1967-68?

2. What Rhode Island player broke Hank Luisetti's collegiate career scoring record with his 1730th point in 1942?

3. Only one backcourt man has led the ABA in scoring. Name him.

4. Wilt Chamberlain scored 100 points in a game against New York in 1962. What was the second highest point total by an NBA player and who had it?

5. What Temple player was the first major college player in modern times to score more than 70 points in one game?

6. Who holds the record of 78 points for most points scored by a guard in an NBA game?

7. Frank Selvy of Furman holds the major college record of 100 points in a single game. Against what team did he set it?

8. Who holds the record for most points scored in an NBA playoff game?

9. What West Texas State player set a single season scoring record of 520 points (17 points a game) during the 1941-42 season?

10. It wasn't until 1960 that the NBA scoring champ averaged more than 30 points a game. Name him.

11. Three major college players averaged more than 30 points a game in 1953-54, the first time that many did so. Name them.

12. Who was the Oklahoma A&M player who set a national record of 58 points in a game against St. Louis in 1946?

13. Who has the highest scoring average in NBA playoff games?

14. Who holds the record for most points in an NCAA tournament game?

15. What Kansas player was the first to average more than 30 points a game in the NCAA tournament when he did it in 1952?

113. Teams of Glory

Some college teams are distinguished by nicknames that denote their style of play, their determination, or their success. Match the nicknames with the schools

1. Seven Mules
2. Vow Boys
3. Iron Men
4. Golden Avalanche
5. Chinese Bandits
6. Praying Colonels
7. Aerial Circus
8. Wonder Bears
9. Flaming Sophomores
10. Blocks of Granite

a) Centre College
b) Tennessee
c) California
d) Notre Dame
e) Stanford
f) Fordham
g) Brown
h) Marquette
i) Louisiana State
j) Southern Methodist

114. The Winter Olympics

1. When and where were the first Winter Olympics held?

2. Who was the Austrian skier who won three gold medals at Cortina, Italy, in 1956?

3. Who was the American who won gold medals in men's figure skating in 1948 and 1952?

4. Who was the first American woman to win a gold medal in the Winter Olympics when she took the slalom in 1948?

5. Who was the goaltender on the American hockey team which upset the Russians and won the Olympic gold medal at Squaw Valley in 1960?

6. Who were the brothers who won the gold medal for the U.S. in the two-man bobsled competition in the 1932 Games at Lake Placid?

7. Who was the first American woman to win a figure skating gold medal?

8. Two American men won all four speed skating events in 1932, the only such American sweep in history. Name them.

9. Who was the only American to win two gold medals in skiing?

10. Who was the man who won a boxing gold medal in the 1920 Olympics and received another as a member of the winning American four-man bobsled team in 1932?

115. Moving Up

These major league baseball players were outstanding small-college players. Match them with their schools.

1.	Ralph Garr	a)	Lewis (Ill.)
2.	Joe Niekro	b)	Eastern Illinois
3.	Steve Barber	c)	Claremont-Mudd (Calif.)'
4.	Ray Washburn	d)	Western Washington
5.	Jim Fairey	e)	LaVerne (Calif.)
6.	Ed Speizio	f)	Iowa Wesleyan
7.	Wes Parker	g)	West Liberty (W.Va.)
8.	Dave Lopes	h)	Carson-Newman (Tenn.)
9.	Marty Pattin	i)	Erskine (S.C.)
10.	Roger Repoz	j)	Grambling (La.)
11.	Clyde Wright	k)	Whitworth (Wash.)

116. On the Line

The center and two wings on a hockey team's attacking line often form a devastating combination and earn a special nickname. Who were on

1. Boston's Kraut Line?
2. Detroit's Production Line?
3. Montreal's Punch Line?
4. Toronto's Kid Line?
5. Chicago's Hem Line?
6. New York's Gag Line?

117. Cinders and Sawdust

1. On May 6, 1954, he became the first man to run a mile in less than four minutes when he was timed in 3:59.4. Name him.

2. Who was the first man to run 100 yards in 9.1 seconds, in 1963?

3. Between 1908 and 1964 only one American won an Olympic running event 1500 meters or longer. What was the event and who won the medal in 1952?

4. Who was the first American to run a mile in less than four minutes when he ran a 3:58.7?

5. Who was the first pole vaulter to clear 15 feet?

6. Who was the world-record setting shot putter who was one of Louisiana State's five-man team that won the NCAA team title in 1933?

7. What University of Nebraska sprinter set world records in the 220-yard and 200-meter dashes in 1926 that stood for a decade until Jesse Owens broke them?

8. Who was the first high jumper to clear 7 feet?

9. When Jim Ryun ran the mile in 3:51.3 in 1966 he became the first American to hold the record in three decades. Who was the last American before Ryun to hold the mark?

10. Who was the first pole vaulter to clear 16 feet, in 1962?

118. Voices

Match the announcers on the left with the event that they are commonly associated with on the right.

1. Graham McNamee
2. Clem McCarthy
3. Don Dunphy
4. Mel Allen
5. Joe Boland

a) Notre Dame football
b) Friday night fights
c) First Rose Bowl broadcast
d) Kentucky Derby
e) World Series

119. Distinctive

Some basketball players were so unique that they earned special nicknames. Who were.

1. The Jet
2. The Pearl
3. The Horse
4. The Big O
5. The Big Dipper
6. The Hill

120. Aerialists

Which of these quarterbacks never threw seven touchdown passes in a game?

a) John Unitas
b) Y. A. Tittle
c) Sid Luckman

121. Pitchers at Bat

1. What American Leaguer holds both the career and single season records for home runs by a pitcher (37 and 9, respectively)?

2. What Atlanta pitcher hit two grand slam home runs in one game during the 1966 season?

3. What National League pitcher came to bat a total of seventy times during the 1962 season and failed to get a base hit?

4. Who holds the National League record of thirty-five career home runs by a pitcher?

5. What Chicago Cub pitcher struck out in fourteen consecutive official at-bats in 1968?

6. Only two men have ever been walked twice in the same inning of a World Series game. Who was the Yankee pitcher who received two such passes in the 1937 Series?

7. What Baltimore Oriole is the only pitcher to hit a grand slam home run in the World Series?

8. What St. Louis Cardinal is the only pitcher to get two hits in one inning of a World Series game?

9. Who is the only pitcher to hit a home run in his first time at bat in the World Series when he did it in 1968?

10. Two Dodger pitchers have hit seven home runs in one season, the National League record. Name them.

122. Catchers at Bat

1. What Phillie "Whiz Kid" and Montreal Expo are the only two catchers to hit two home runs in one inning?

2. What Detroit catcher tied the American League record by being hit by a pitched ball 24 times in 1968?

3. Name the catchers who hold their league's records for most home runs in a career.

4. Only one catcher has hit four home runs in a single World Series. Name him.

5. What New York Giant catcher hit a record three sacrifice flies in the four-game 1954 World Series?

6. What Cincinnati catcher set the National League record for grounding into double plays when he hit into 30 in 1938?

7. Two catchers, one Yankee and one Oakland A, hit home runs in their first World Series at-bats. Name them.

8. What Yankee is the only catcher to hit four home runs in consecutive times at bat in two different games?

9. Who holds the major league single season record of 40 home runs by a catcher?

10. Yogi Berra set the American League record of most home runs by a catcher in 1956 with 30. What Baltimore receiver matched that total two years later?

123. First Basemen at Bat

1. Who holds the single season record for most home runs by a first baseman?

2. Who is the only first baseman ever to win the Triple Crown?

3. Who is the last first baseman to hit four home runs in one game?

4. What first baseman had two .400 batting seasons for the St. Louis Cardinals in the 1920s?

5. The single season record in the National League for home runs by a first baseman is 51. Who holds it?

6. The record for most home runs in a five-game World Series is three. What first baseman holds it?

7. The major league record for most hits in consecutive times at bat is twelve. What Detroit first baseman shares this record with Pinky Higgins?

8. What Cardinal first baseman is the only man to drive in 12 runs in a single game?

9. What Dodger first baseman established a rookie record by hitting 28 sacrifice flies in one season?

10. Who holds the American and National League record for most home runs in a career by first basemen?

124. Second Basemen at Bat

1. When Dave Johnson hit 43 home runs in 1973 he broke the all-time record for homers by a second baseman. Who had the old record of 42?

2. What Yankee second baseman came to bat a record eleven times in a 22-inning game in 1962?

3. What National League second baseman had more career home runs, 263, than any other?

4. The same man holds both the American League career and single season records for home runs. Name him.

5. What Dodger second baseman worked out a record 148 walks in 1945?

6. What Detroit second baseman established an American League record by not grounding into a single double play in 570 times at bat in 1968?

7. The Yankees had two second basemen who hit .500 in World Series play. One did it in 1941, the other in 1953. Name them.

8. What St. Louis second baseman set the record for most two-base hits in three consecutive games when he hit eight in 1948?

9. What Hall of Fame second baseman holds the career record of 511 sacrifice flies hit in the American League between 1906 and 1926?

10. What second baseman set the record of 10 doubles in World Series play between 1921 and 1934?

11. Only one second baseman has ever been named a league Most Valuable Player more than once. Who is he?

125. Third Basemen at Bat

1. Who holds the major league record for most home runs in a career by a third baseman?

2. What Giants third baseman hit .474 with his "bottle bat" to lead his team in a four-game sweep of the Yankees in the 1922 World Series?

3. What Cleveland Indian third baseman hit a single season AL record 45 home runs?

4. The American League record for sacrifice flies in a career is held by what third baseman?

5. What two third basemen led the National League in walks seven times between 1961 and 1968?

6. Who is the New York Yankee third baseman who hit a total of seven home runs in World Series competition?

7. Who holds the American League record for home runs by a third baseman in a career?

8. What Chicago Cub third baseman struck out six times in one game in 1956?

9. What New York Yankee third baseman set a modern record by scoring runs in eighteen consecutive games in August of 1939?

10. An eighteen-year-old New York Giant third baseman, substituting for the injured Heinie Groh in the 1924 World Series, hit a record-tying four singles in a game against Washington. Name him.

126. Shortstops at Bat

1. What Pittsburgh Pirate holds the record for best one-season batting average by a shortstop (.385)?

2. The record for fewest hits in a season—minimum 400 times at bat—is 82 in the American League, 90 in the National. Name the shortstops who hold these records.

3. What National Leaguer holds both the single season and career home run records for a shortstop?

4. Only one shortstop has gotten five extra-base hits in a game. Name the Cleveland Indian who did it.

5. Name the National League shortstop who led the league in singles four times between 1960 and 1969.

6. What light-hitting shortstop batted .417 in helping the St. Louis Cardinals beat the Yankees in the 1926 World Series?

7. What American League shortstop led the major leagues in sacrifice flies for four straight years, 1949-52?

8. Two Red Sox hold, respectively, the American League records for most home runs in a single season and in a career by a shortstop. Name them.

9. What National League shortstop led his team in batting in three different World Series after World War II?

10. Who was the American League shortstop who received 100 or more walks six consecutive seasons (1947-52)?

127. Outfielders at Bat

1. What outfielder holds the National League record for most home runs in a season (56)?

2. What American League outfielder holds the all-time record for runs scored with 2,244?

3. What outfielder received more intentional walks in his career than any other player?

4. What San Francisco outfielder was the only rookie to hit a grand slam home run in his first major league game?

5. What well-traveled American League outfielder hit a record 793 doubles in his career during the first third of this century?

6. What Boston Brave holds the National League record for consecutive-game hitting streak by an outfielder with 37?

7. What Yankee outfielder batted .438, hit three home runs, and drove in six runs to help New York sweep the 1938 World Series in four games?

8. What Pittsburgh Pirate right fielder set a league record by getting 10 hits in two consecutive games?

9. What Yankee outfielder has the highest batting average (.625) for a World Series regular?

10. Two outfielders, a Dodger in 1952 and a Cardinal in 1968, share the hitting record of 24 total bases in a World Series. Name them.

128. College Connection

Some basketball players develop such a strong identification with the city where they play professionally that their college affiliation is forgotten. Match these men and their schools.

1. Bill Sharman
2. Bailey Howell
3. Elgin Baylor
4. Jack Twyman
5. Dave Gambee
6. Gene Shue
7. Johnny Green
8. Red Rocha
9. Paul Seymour
10. Don Ohl
11. Wilt Chamberlain
12. Neil Johnston
13. Adrian Smith
14. Slater Martin
15. Wayne Embry
16. Jim Luscutoff
17. Bob Ferry
18. Ray Scott
19. Larry Foust
20. Johnny Kerr
21. George Yardley

a) Oregon
b) Illinois
c) Ohio State
d) Portland
e) Seattle
f) Michigan State
g) Illinois
h) Kentucky
i) Kansas
j) Maryland
k) Texas
l) Miami (O.)
m) St. Louis
n) Stanford
o) Oregon State
p) LaSalle
q) Southern California
r) Toledo
s) Cincinnati
t) Oregon State
u) Mississippi State

129. Heisman Trophy

1. Army's Doc Blanchard and Glenn Davis won the Heisman Trophy as college football player of the year in 1945 and 1946, respectively. The only other time two men from the same school won it in consecutive years was 1936 and 1937. Name the two Yale players who earned it.

2. Besides Davis and Blanchard, what other Army man won the Heisman?

3. Name the four Ohio State winners.

4. Who was the last Ivy League player to win it?

5. More players from Notre Dame have won the Heisman than from any other school. Name the six.

6. Who are the four players from Texas schools to win the Heisman?

7. Since 1960, only four juniors have won the Heisman. Name them.

8. Who was the Michigan running back who won the trophy in 1940?

9. Name the four Southern California Trojans who have won the Heisman.

10. Excluding Ivy Leaguers, only one player from a New England college has ever won the Heisman Trophy. Name him.

130. Switch

Several of today's colleges and universities gained a measure of athletic fame in the past under a different name. Give these schools' past identities.

1. Oklahoma State
2. Maryland-Eastern Shore
3. Texas-El Paso
4. Tennessee State
5. Auburn

131. Long-range Bombers

Which of these quarterbacks never passed for 500 yards in a game?

    a) Norm Van Brocklin
    b) Y. A. Tittle
    c) Joe Namath

132. Actors As Athletes

1. Who played Jimmy Piersall in *Fear Strikes Out*?

2. Who played Dizzy Dean in *The Pride of St. Louis*?

3. Who played Jim Thorpe in *Jim Thorpe—All-American*?

4. Who played Rocky Graziano in *Somebody Up There Likes Me*?

5. Who played Monte Stratton in *The Monte Stratton Story*?

6. Who played Lou Gehrig in *Pride of the Yankees*?

133. Taking a Turn

1. In 1961, who was the switch-hitter who collected a record 24 pinch-hits for the Baltimore Orioles?

2. What pitcher ended his twenty-two-year career with a total of 58 pinch-hits?

3. Who were the two players who batted .419 as pinch-batters in 1962, one as a utility man for the Orioles, the other with the New York Mets?

4. Playing in the 1930s and '40s, what outfielder-third baseman had a career batting average of .312 as a pinch-hitter?

5. Who is the National Leaguer who collected 18 home runs as a pinch-batter between 1954 and 1966?

6. After starting with the Cardinals, this switch-hitter moved to New York and Milwaukee before returning to St. Louis, where he led the league with 22 pinch-hits in 1962. Name him.

7. Who is the right-handed hitter who spent most of his career in the 1920s and '30s with Detroit, collecting 76 hits in 253 pinch-hitting appearances for a .300 average?

8. Who is the pinch-batter who played for the Yankees and Senators in 1961, when he appeared in a record eighty-one games and collected 14 hits and 18 walks?

9. Who was the Dodger who had only nine pinch-hits in all of 1932, but six of which were home runs?

10. Playing for the Cardinals and Cubs in the late 1940s and early '50s, who is the left-handed batter who knocked three grand slam home runs as a pinch-batter?

11. Who appeared in seventy-seven games with the White Sox in 1967 and was a pinch-hitter in every one of those games?

134. Linked to College

Match the professional golfers with the colleges they attended.

1.	Arnold Palmer	a)	Alabama
2.	Miller Barber	b)	Stanford
3.	Don January	c)	Texas A&M
4.	Jack Nicklaus	d)	Duke
5.	Gardiner Dickenson	e)	Houston
6.	Bobby Nicols	f)	San Diego State
7.	Art Wall	g)	San Jose State
8.	Dow Finsterwald	h)	Holy Cross
9.	Frank Beard	i)	Wake Forest
10.	Bob Roseburg	j)	Southern California
11.	Ken Venturi	k)	Arkansas
12.	Gene Littler	l)	Ohio University
13.	Paul Harney	m)	North Texas State
14.	Dave Stockton	n)	Florida
15.	Homero Blancas	o)	Ohio State

135. Guys Named Joe

Identify

1. Jumpin' Joe
2. Joltin' Joe
3. Broadway Joe
4. Jersey Joe
5. Shoeless Joe

136. Sugar Bowl

1. In the 1952 Sugar Bowl, Maryland beat Tennessee, 28-13, with the winners' Mighty Mo being named the game's outstanding player. Who was "Mighty Mo"?

2. The last time anyone played a full sixty minutes in a Sugar Bowl game was in 1947, when two backfield men for Georgia did it against North Carolina. Name these Bulldog stars.

3. In 1963 a Mississippi quarterback threw for a record 242 yards and picked up another 15 rushing for a total-offense record against Arkansas. Name this Rebel.

4. The 1957 Sugar Bowl saw a future NFL pass-receiving star with MVP honors by picking up 88 yards rushing in 14 carries as he led Baylor to a 13-7 victory over Tennessee. Name the Bear.

5. Although Alabama lost to Duke (29-26) in 1946, the star of the game was what eighteen-year-old quarterback for the Crimson Tide?

6. National champion Oklahoma was upset, 13-7, by Kentucky, led by Vito "Babe" Parilli in 1951. Who was the Wildcat lineman who was voted the game's outstanding player?

7. Alabama beat Ole Miss, 12-7, in 1964 on four field goals by whom?

8. In 1934, the Texas Christian quarterback completed 17 of 27 passes to lead the Horned Frogs to a 15-7 victory over Carnegie Tech. Name the TCU passer.

9. Boston College, coached by Frank Leahy, beat Tennessee, coached by Bob Neyland, 14-13, in the 1941 Sugar Bowl. Who was the skinny BC quarterback who scored the winning touchdown?

10. Alabama crushed Nebraska (34-7) in the 1967 game. Who were the 'Bama quarterback and end who led the onslaught?

137. Match Race

Horse racing's ultimate test is a match race in which there are only two horses in the running, a winner and a loser. Which was the winner in these encounters?

1. Coaltown vs. Capot at Pimlico in 1949
2. Armed vs. Assault at Belmont Park in 1947

3. Whirlaway vs. Alsab at Narragansett Park in 1942
4. Nashua vs. Swaps at Washington Park in 1955
5. Seabiscuit vs. War Admiral at Pimlico in 1938

138. Home Ice

Minor league hockey teams have attracted a loyal following in many cities. Identify these teams with their nicknames.

1. Baltimore	a) Reds
2. Hershey	b) Americans
3. Providence	c) Gulls
4. Rochester	d) Buckaroos
5. Phoenix	e) Totems
6. Seattle	f) Bears
7. Portland	g) Roadrunners
8. San Diego	h) Clippers

139. NCAA Hoop Championships

1. Between 1948 and 1951, Kentucky became the first school to win three NCAA championships. Whom did they beat for their three titles?

2. Who were the starters on UCLA's team in Lew Alcindor's sophomore season (1967)?

3. Indiana beat Kansas, 69-68, for the 1953 crown, but what member of the losing team was named MVP?

4. The 1940-41 season was the 50th anniversary of the invention of basketball. Who won the NCAA title that season?

5. Loyola of Chicago used only five men in beating Cincinnati, 60-58, in 1963. Name the five.

6. Who beat San Francisco early in the 1954-55 season to prevent the Bill Russell-led Dons from becoming the first unbeaten NCAA champion that season?

7. Who was the star of Oklahoma A&M's 1946 squad that was the first team to win two NCAA crowns?

8. What NCAA champion had the worst won-lost record?

9. What team was eliminated from the NIT, but then received a bid for the NCAA and went on to win it in 1944?

10. Who did North Carolina beat in successive triple-overtime games to win the NCAA honors in 1957?

11. Who were the five starters on the 1966 NCAA title winner, the team that interrupted UCLA's string?

12. Name the player who won the MVP award in 1956 although his team won only the consolation game.

13. Which were the only two schools from the same state to play for the championship?

14. Which were the only two schools to play each other in consecutive championship games?

140. Pugilists

1. What was the smallest crowd that paid to see a heavyweight championship fight?

2. Who was the oldest heavyweight champion?

3. Four men retired as "the undefeated heavyweight champion of the world." Only two stayed retired and unbeaten; who were they?

4. What fight drew the greatest paid, in-person attendance?

5. Who was the tallest heavyweight champion?

6. Who was the youngest heavyweight champion?

7. Which of these countries was never the site of a heavyweight championship fight: Australia, Cuba, Spain, Italy, Germany?

8. What was the largest crowd to see a heavyweight title fight indoors?

9. Who were the heaviest men to fight for the title in one bout?

10. Who was the shortest heavyweight champion?

11. Who was the lightest heavyweight champion?

12. Five men who were, at one time or another, heavyweight champions were knocked out by Joe Louis during his career. Name them.

141. Launch

Many professional football stars have developed their skills in small schools. Match these players with the colleges they attended.

1. Harlon Hill
2. Dutch Clark
3. Arnie Herber
4. Joe Perry
5. Alex Sandusky
6. Johnny Blood
7. Larry Hand
8. Roosevelt Brown
9. Clark Hinkle
10. Jack Kemp
11. Clyde Turner
12. Cliff Battles
13. Willie Gallimore
14. Tony Canadeo
15. Dan Towler
16. Carl Taseff
17. Fuzzy Thurston
18. Dick Lane
19. Andy Robustelli
20. Steve Owen

a) Appalachian State (N.C.)
b) Florida A&M
c) Morgan State (Md.)
d) Gonzaga (Wash.)
e) Bucknell (Pa.)
f) Washington & Jefferson (Pa.)
g) Phillips (Okla.)
h) John Carroll (O.)
i) Arnold (Conn.)
j) St. John's (Minn.)
k) Valparaiso (Ind.)
l) Scotsbluff Jr. College
m) Clarion (Pa.)
n) Compton Jr. College
o) West Virginia Wesleyan
p) Regis (Colo.)
q) Hardin-Simmons (Tex.)
r) Colorado College
s) Occidental (Calif.)
t) Florence (Ala.)

142. Athletes As Actors

1. What heavyweight champion starred in *All the Young Men*?

2. What football-player-turned-actor played Spear Chucker in the movie version of *M*A*S*H*?

3. Television's Rifleman, Chuck Connors, played with what big league teams in baseball and basketball?

4. What NFL wide receiver quit football to make his film debut in *The Guns of the Magnificent Seven*?

5. What heavyweight champion was the star of the Broadway musical version of *Big Time Buck White*?

6. What football quarterback starred in *Norwood* and *C. C. and Company*?

143. Long-time Throwng

Which of these quarterbacks threw for the most yardage in his pro career?

    a) John Brodie
    b) Fran Tarkenton
    c) Sonny Jurgenson

144. In the U.S. Open

1. Who has the lowest 72-hole score of 272 in U.S. Open play?

2. In 1939 there were three men tied at 284. Two of the three then tied in an 18-hole playoff. Who was the winner after another 18 holes of golf?

3. The leading money winner of 1952 earned a total of $37,032.97, including a winner's share of the U.S. Open prize money. Name him.

4. The lowest one-round score in Open play is 63. Name the three who share the record.

5. Who was the golfer who carded a 19 on the par 4 16th hole of the Cherry Hills Course in Denver, Colorado, in the 1938 Open?

6. Who was the Cinderella winner of the 1955 Open?

7. There have been 26 playoffs in the U.S. Open. Who was the only one to twice win a playoff?

8. The 1950 Open required a playoff to determine the winner. Lloyd Mangrum and George Fazio lost in the playoff. Who won?

9. Only five amateurs have won the U.S. Open. Name them.

10. What was the closest Sam Snead came to winning the Open?

145. Roundball Mentors

Coaches and their reputations live well past their eras, especially in the rapidly changing game of basketball. Some of these coaches may be "before your time," but their long stands in college and the innovations they developed have left their mark on the game. Make the matches.

1. Joe Mullaney
2. John Bunn
3. Forest "Phog" Allen
4. Tony Hinkle
5. Arad McCutchan
6. George Ireland
7. Phil Woolpert
8. Branch McCracken
9. "Bones" McKinney
10. Joe Lapchick
11. Hank Iba
12. Ed Diddle
13. Nat Holman
14. Clair Bee
15. Doc Carlson
16. Fred Taylor
17. Peck Hickman
18. Slats Gill
19. Ev Case
20. Taps Gallagher
21. Jim Snyder
22. Frank Keaney
23. Tom Blackburn
24. Lucias Mitchell
25. "Honey" Russell
26. Al Severance

a) San Francisco
b) Western Kentucky
c) St. John's (N.Y.)
d) Providence
e) Louisville
f) City College of New York
g) Oregon State
h) Ohio University
i) Dayton
j) Seton Hall
k) Evansville
l) Stanford
m) Pittsburgh
n) Kentucky State
o) Rhode Island
p) Butler
q) Niagara
r) Villanova
s) Indiana
t) Long Island University
u) Kansas
v) North Carolina State
w) Loyola (Chicago)
x) Wake Forest
y) Oklahoma State
z) Ohio State

146. Beyond Their Sports

Many competitors with distinctive nicknames had large followings that extended beyond their sport. Identify these.

1. What jockey was known as "The Iceman"?

2. What figure skater was called the "Norwegian Doll"?

3. Who was the wrestler of the 1920s known as "Strangler"?

4. What golfer was referred to as "Champagne Tony"?

5. Who was the boxer they called "Gentleman Jim"?

6. What miler was called "The Flying Parson"?

7. Who was the globetrotting basketball player known as "Goose"?

8. What female tennis star of the 1950s was called "Little Mo"?

147. Play on Names

A style of play often gave basketball players a nickname. Who were

1. Tricky Dick
2. Jumpin' Joe
3. Easy Ed
4. Jungle Jim
5. Hot Rod

148. AFL History

1. Where were the teams and what were their nicknames when the AFL began its first season?

2. Who kicked the sixth-quarter field goal that gave Dallas a 20-17 victory in the 1962 season's championship game?

3. What two players played in every single game their teams were in between 1960 and 1973?

4. Denver and Boston played in the first AFL regular season game on September 9, 1960. Who won?

5. Who was the last rookie to lead the AFL in rushing. Name him.

6. Of the teams in the AFL from 1960 through 1969, which had the most victories?

7. Which of the original eight AFL teams had the worst record before the merger with the NFL?

8. Which of the original AFL teams had the fewest losses in the ten years of the league's existence?

9. Which team had the best record in the East?

10. Which of the charter members had the worst record in the East?

149. On the Record

Many baseball players were best known by their nicknames. Supply the given names of

1. Dizzy Dean
2. Whitey Ford
3. Arky Vaughn
4. Rube Walker
5. Pepper Martin
6. Vinegar Bend Mizell
7. Minnie Minoso
8. Red Schoendienst
9. Zack Taylor
10. Lefty Grove
11. Duke Snider
12. Pie Traynor
13. Peanuts Lowrey
14. Rabbit Maranville
15. Babe Ruth

a) James Wren
b) Edward Charles
c) Wilmer David
d) George Herman
e) Jay Hanna
f) Edwin Donald
g) Harold Joseph
h) Joseph Floyd
i) Harry Lee
j) Walter James Vincent
k) Saturnino Orestes Arrieta Armas
l) Albert Bluford
m) Johnny Leonard Roosevelt
n) Albert Fred
o) Robert Moses

150. Back to College

Some college basketball stars return to their alma maters to coach. Identify these men who did just that:

1. This Canisius star led the Griffins to a 17-8 record in 1950 before returning to Buffalo to coach in 1961.

2. An Eastern Kentucky graduate, he played with the New York Knicks in the 1950s before guiding the Maroons.

3. This high-scoring Furman guard coached the Paladins from 1967 through 1970.

4. This former West Virginia player developed Hot Rod Hundley and Jerry West as a coach in Morgantown.

5. This Stanford coach played on the Cardinal five that won the NCAA tournament in 1942.

6. As a player, this coach teamed with Walter Dukes in leading Seton Hall to the NIT title in 1953.

7. He led LaSalle to national honors as a player and coached there two years.

8. This coach is best remembered for a 55-foot shot he made for Rhode Island in the NIT.

9. This Bronco player spent time playing professionally in Oshkosh and Washington before returning to coach Santa Clara in 1951.

10. This Fordham Ram led the nation in rebounding in 1953 and 15 years later returned to the Bronx to coach for a couple of seasons.

151. By the Numbers

1. Who was the halfback who made No. 77 famous in the 1920s?

2. What high-scoring basketball player had no fear of No. 13?

3. What baseball pitcher wore No. 96 on his uniform?

4. What football center wore No. 00?

5. Who was the early NBA superstar who wore No. 99?

152. Doubling Up

Match the major league ballplayer on the left with his double identity, or nickname, on the right.

1. James O. Carlton		a)	Red
2. Jesse Haines		b)	Stubby
3. Spurgeon Ferdinand Chandler		c)	Pumpsie
4. George Dauss		d)	Bump
5. Sylvester Urban Donnally		e)	Spud
6. Hollis Thurston		f)	Frenchy
7. James A. Collins		g)	Mule
8. Jerry Dean Gibbs		h)	Doc
9. James Francis Hogan		i)	Sloppy
10. John Blake		j)	Ping
11. Charles Lucas		k)	Chief
12. Alvin Floyd Crowder		l)	Bubba
13. Irving Darius Hadley		m)	Catfish
14. George Metkovich		n)	Jake
15. Frank Overmire		o)	Ripper
16. Roger Cramer		p)	Shanty
17. Frank Bodie		q)	Tex
18. Stanley Bordagaray		r)	Sheriff
19. Elijah Green		s)	Hooks
20. George Haas		t)	Blix
21. Emory Church		u)	Pop
22. Charles Albert Bender		v)	General

153. Varsity Varieties

Identify these collegiate football players by their nicknames.

1. A California boy who went east to the U.S. Military Academy, where he set a school rushing record as the Cadets' Mr. Outside.

2. The other half of Army's devastating combination of the mid-1940s who was called Mr. Inside.

3. The Wisconsin pass receiver and runner who had a peculiar style which earned him the nickname of Crazylegs.

4. The diminutive Yale halfback who was known both as the Mighty Atom and Little Boy Blue.

5. As regular as a railroad train and almost as powerful, the North Carolina runner known as "Choo Choo."

6. A scrambling style earned this Navy quarterback the sobriquet Roger the Dodger.

7. Orenthal James were his given names, but this speedy Southern California halfback was often called Orange Juice.

8. Running with abandon earned this Ohio State halfback the nickname of Hopalong.

9. Who was the Monk who played halfback for the outstanding Tulane teams of the mid-1930s?

10. Who was the Georgia Fireball who scored the Bulldogs' only touchdown in the 9-0 Rose Bowl victory in 1943?

154. Tag Lines

Teams often gain additional nicknames during a season or era because of a distinctive achievement or manner of play. Match the teams on the left with their extra nicknames.

1. Wonder Five
2. Hitless Wonders
3. Whiz Kids
4. Murderers Row
5. Monsters of the Midway

a) New York Yankees
b) Chicago Bears
c) St. John's University
d) Chicago White Sox
e) Illinois

155. Blasters

Which two of these players never hit four home runs in a game?

a) Gil Hodges
b) Henry Aaron
c) Babe Ruth
d) Lou Gehrig
e) Willie Mays

156. Hoops—NAIA Style

1. Only two schools have won three consecutive NAIA championships. Name them.

2. Who was the skinny 6'8" center called "Twiggy" who earned NAIA tournament honors in leading Oklahoma Baptist to the championship in 1966 and second place the following year?

3. What NBA all-star forward from Guilford College set a NAIA regular-season career record for field goal accuracy, making 64 percent of his shots?

4. Prairie View A&M has been to the NAIA tournament only once, and won that year (1962). Who was the center who grabbed a record 96 rebounds and earned MVP honors for the Panthers?

5. Who was the 6'9" center who average 48.3 points a game in 1953 to establish the all-time regular season career scoring record?

6. Who is the NBA center from Grambling who made a record 21 of 23 free throws in the 1964 tournament?

7. McNeese State is one of the few schools that has won every NAIA tournament game it has played in. Who was the team high scorer and tournament MVP who led the Cowboys to the championship in 1956?

8. What Pan-American forward, who later played in the NBA, averaged 25 points a game in leading the Broncs to the tournament three straight years (1962-64)?

9. Who set the all-time single season scoring record with 1,329 points while he played at Winston-Salem College?

10. Who was the tournament MVP in 1958 and 1959 who led Tennessee State to the championship before going on to star in the ABL and NBA?

157. Big League Rookies

1. Two National Leaguers share the record of thirty-eight home runs by a rookie. Name them.

2. Who was the rookie who batted .403 in forty-one games during the stretch to help Milwaukee win the pennant in 1957?

3. What Cleveland pitcher holds the record of 245 for most strikeouts by a rookie?

4. What St. Louis Cardinal batted a record .373 in his rookie season of 1930?

5. Who holds the major league record of 145 runs batted in during a rookie season, set in 1939?

6. Only five rookies since 1930 have pitched two consecutive shutouts at the start of the major league careers. Name them.

7. What rookie batted .500 and stole five bases to help the St. Louis Cardinals win the 1931 World Series?

8. Two men, one in each league, struck out a record 152 times during their rookie seasons. Name the Red Sox and Phillie players who did it.

9. The modern rookie record for stolen bases in one season is 71. Who set the mark in 1981?

10. Four men have pitched one-hitters in their first major league start. Cleveland's Addie Joss did it in 1902. Name the three others who have done it, all since World War II.

158. AFL Stars

Match these stars of the old American Football League with the schools they attended.

1.	Lionel Taylor	a)	Miami (Fla.)
2.	Gino Cappelletti	b)	North Texas State
3.	Don Maynard	c)	Bluffton College
4.	Clemon Daniels	d)	Cincinnati
5.	Jack Spikes	e)	The Citadel
6.	Ron Mix	f)	Washington
7.	Ernie Ladd	g)	Washington State
8.	Charlie Hennigan	h)	San Jose State
9.	Bill Mathis	i)	Southern California
10.	Tom Sestak	j)	Oregon State
11.	Jim Otto	k)	Texas Christian
12.	Elbert Dubenion	l)	Lamar State
13.	Paul Maguire	m)	Prairie View
14.	Ben Davidson	n)	McNeese State
15.	Art Powell	o)	Texas Western
16.	Paul Lowe	p)	Clemson
17.	Bobby Jancik	q)	Minnesota
18.	Abner Haynes	r)	Northwest Louisiana
19.	Jacky Lee	s)	New Mexico Highlands
20.	Keith Lincoln	t)	Grambling

159. Sticking Handles

1. Who is the "Busher" who was a leading NHL scorer with the Toronto Maple Leafs?

2. Whose name was "Mud"?

3. Who were the "Cat" and the "Black Cat"?

4. No matter what happened, who was the Toronto defenseman who was always "Happy"?

5. Who was the Boston defenseman who had a nickname that sounded like a telegraph message?

6. What Calder Trophy winner was called "Cully"?

7. Who is the "Babe" who played a strong offense as a defenseman with the Rangers and the Maple Leafs?

8. Who was the Montreal Maroon left winger who had very few "hairy" experiences?

9. With a nickname like "Black Jack," who was the Detroit all-league defenseman of the 1940s?

10. A two-time scoring champ in the 1930s with the New York Americans, this man's real first name was David. What was his nickname?

160. The PGA

1. Who won the first Professional Golfers Association tournament in 1916?

2. Who is the only man to win four consecutive PGA championships?

3. The scoring changed from match play to stroke play in 1958. Who won the first tournament under the new system?

4. The largest margin of victory in match play was 8 holes up with 7 left to play. Who beat Sam Snead by this score in 1938?

5. The 1964 PGA tourney was held on Jack Nicklaus' home course in Columbus, Ohio, but the Golden Bear didn't win. Who did?

6. The longest match in PGA history was 43 holes in 1932. Who defeated Walter Hagan in this first-round marathon?

7. There have been five playoffs in PGA tourney history. Name the five playoff winners.

8. Has Arnold Palmer ever won the PGA?

9. Name the only brothers who have won the PGA (in 1957 and 1960).

10. In addition to Walter Hagan, three other men have won the PGA in consecutive years. Name the winners in 1921-22, 1928-29, and 1957-60.

161. Small Rewards

Many basketball players gained a national reputation even though they played basketball for smaller schools. Match the players and their colleges.

1. Norm Hankins	a) Loyola (Md.)
2. Bevo Francis	b) Alderson-Broaddus
3. Frank Selvy	c) West Texas State
4. "Stutz" Modzelewski	d) Denver
5. Joe Miller	e) St. Francis (Pa.)
6. Al Tucker	f) Lawrence Tech
7. Vince Boryla	g) Rio Grande
8. Price Brookfield	h) Rhode Island State
9. Jim Lacy	i) Furman
10. Maurice Stokes	j) Oklahoma Baptist

Answers

1.

1. Red Grange
2. Alan Ameche
3. Jack Manders
4. Lou Groza
5. Dan Towler
6. Eddie LeBaron
7. Gene Lipscomb
8. Dick Lane
9. John McNally
10. Norm Van Brocklin

2.

1. Jimmy Foxx
2. Rogers Hornsby
3. Ty Cobb
4. Charles Nichols
5. Babe Ruth
6. Harry Brecheen
7. Harvey Haddix
8. Harry Walker
9. Leo Durocher
10. Calvin Griffith
11. Ted Williams
12. Frankie Frisch
13. Stan Musial
14. Cornelius McGillicuddy (Connie Mack)
15. John Evers
16. Lou Gehrig
17. Carl Furillo
18. Harry Agganis
19. Roger Bresnahan
20. Adolfo Luque
21. Dom DiMaggio

3.

1. John F. Kennedy, Harvard
2. Woodrow Wilson
3. Dwight D. Eisenhower, as a cadet at West Point
4. William Howard Taft
5. Richard M. Nixon, Whittier

4.

1-a, 2-r, 3-m, 4-q, 5-u, 6-i, 7-l, 8-t, 9-p, 10-h, 11-o, 12-b, 13-e, 14-s, 15-d, 16-f, 17-k, 18-g, 19-c, 20-j, 23-n

5.

1. Dolph Schayes
2. Walter Dukes
3. Elmore Smith, 1971
4. Wilt Chamberlain, 55, against Boston, November 24, 1960
5. Tom Gola
6. Nate Thurmond and Jerry Lucas
7. Charlie Slack, 25.6
8. Bailey Howell and Walter Dukes
9. Ernie Beck
10. Maurice Stokes, 1957, with Rochester

6.

1. Glenn Hall, Bobby Hull, Stan Mikita, Pierre Pilote, Ken Wharram
2. George (Buck), Frank, Billy, Bob

3. Dit Clapper
4. Wayne Cashman, Phil Esposito, Ken Hodge
5. Detroit defenseman Bill Hollett
6. Elmer Lach and Toe Blake
7. Frank Boucher
8. Alex Delvecchio
9. Bill Mosienko
10. Marty Barry

7.

1-c, 2-l, 3-o, 4-g, 4-m, 6-e, 7-n, 8-d, 9-j, 10-a, 11-b, 12-h, 13-i, 14-k, 15-f

8.

1-e, 2-l, 3-g, 4-i, 5-n, 6-o, 7-q, 8-c, 9-b, 10-r, 11-s, 12-u, 13-v, 14-k, 15-f, 16-t, 17-p, 18-m, 19-d, 20-j, 21-a, 22-h

9.

1. Horton Smith
2. Gay Brewer
3. Ken Venturi
4. Cary Middlecoff
5. Frank Stranahan
6. Jack Nicklaus
7. Jack Nicklaus
8. Doug Ford
9. Byron Nelson
10. Billy Joe Patton

10.

1. Mike Henry
2. Clarence "Buster" Crabbe
3. Johnny Weissmuller
4. Glenn Morris
5. Don Bragg

11.

c

12.

1-b, e, or g; 2-e or g; 3-a or d; 4-h; 5-b; 6-j; 7-i; 8-d; 9-f; 10-c

13.

1. Emil "Bus" Mosbacher
2. T. O. M. Sopwith
3. Five
4. A schooner named *America*, representing the United States, won the 100 Guinea Cup in the Isle of Wright race in 1851, and the Cup was renamed for the *America*
5. Canada
6. Harold S. Vanderbilt

14.

1. Bobby Riggs
2. Don Budge and Rod Laver (twice)
3. John Newcombe and Tony Roche beat Ken Rosewall and Fred Stolle
4. Pancho Gonzales

    5. Bill Tilden
    6. Charles Pasarell and Ron Holmberg
    7. Dennis Ralston
    8. Jack Kramer
    9. Arthur Ashe
  10. Don Budge

15.

1-c, 2-d, 3-e, 4-a, 5-b

16.

1-y, 2-k, 3-m, 4-i, 5-q, 6-w, 7-r, 8-v, 9-zz, 10-h or j,
11-n, 12-g, 13-z, 14-s, 15-c, 16-b, 17-b or l, 18-e, 19-t,
20-d, 21-p, 22-u, 23-a or b, 24-f, 25-y or j, 26-x, 27-o

17.

    1. eleven years, 8 months, 9 days
    2. James J. Braddock, June 22, 1937, in Chicago
    3. Louis retired unbeaten on March 1, 1949
    4. twenty-five times
    5. Arturo Godoy, Buddy Baer, Abe Simon, Billy
       Conn, Jersey Joe Walcott
    6. Victims of Louis, they belonged to the "Bum
       of the Month Club"
    7. Lexington, Alabama
    8. Ezzard Charles
    9. San Francisco
  10. Arthur Donovan

18.

1. Ann Curtis
2. Bill Bradley and Bill Walton
3. Bill Toomey
4. Glenn Cunningham, 1933; Bill Bonthron, 1934
5. Dick Button
6. Wilma Rudolph
7. Cornelius Warmerdam
8. Lawson Little, 1935
9. Marathon runner Frank Shorter
10. Don Budge, 1937

19.

1. Babe Herman
2. Lew Burdette
3. Ernie Lombardi
4. Joe Pepitone
5. Fred Merkle
6. Mickey Owens
7. Charlie Root

20.

1. Steve Van Buren and O. J. Simpson
2. Dick Lynch's
3. Ernie Nevers
4. Tank Younger, Grambling
5. Otto Graham, five
6. Jim Brown, Syracuse
7. Terry Brennan and Emil Sitko
8. Cliff Battles
9. Pervis Atkins, Bob Gaiters, James "Preacher" Pilot
10. Marion Motley

21.

1. Ernie Calverley's
2. George Linn
3. Les Selvage, Anaheim
4. Darrel Carrier
5. Jerry West

22.

c

23.

1. Gordie Howe, 22
2. Wayne Gretzky, 4 in 1983
3. Eric Nesterenko, 3 in 1961
4. Walley Hergesheimer
5. Glenn Hall, 13
6. Wales, 7, Campbell 6, 1984
7. Ted Lindsay, 1950; Gordie Howe, 1965; Pete Mahovlich, 1976; Wayne Gretzky, 1983; Don Maloney, 1984
8. Dennis Ververgaert
9. Mark Messier
10. Jacques Plante

24.

1. kissing your sister
2. the tough get going
3. finish last
4. hit to right
5. but how you play the game
6. one leg at a time

7. at a time
8. until the last man is out
9. a prayer
10. they ain't
11. no hit

25.

1. Louis Mayer, 1928, 1933, 1936
2. 74.07 mph
3. Jimmy Clarke
4. Miller Eight
5. Bill Vukovich, 1953, 1954
6. Boyle Special
7. Rear-engine Lotus-Ford
8. Duesenberg
9. Joe Leonard
10. Mario Andretti, 1969

26.

1. Hal Greer
2. Nile Kinnick
3. Andy Hebenton
4. Steve Garvey
5. Chuck Bednarik
6. John Kerr
7. Pancho Gonzales
8. Walter Johnson and Warren Spahn
9. George Blanda
10. Ty Cobb and Stan Musial, respectively

27.

1. CCNY, 1950
2. Oregon beat Ohio State, 46-33
3. NIT started in 1938, NCAA in 1939
4. Jacksonville, 1969-70

5. Pitt vs. Fordham, from Madison Square Garden on February 28, 1940
6. Wyoming beat St. John's of New York, 52-47
7. San Francisco, 1949
8. Holy Cross, 1947
9. LaSalle beat Bradley, 92-76
10. Holy Cross, 1947

28.

1. Ernie Davis, 1961
2. Cleveland Pipers with John McLendon
3. Althea Gibson, 1957, women's singles
4. Chuck Cooper, Boston; Nat Clifton, New York, 1950
5. Charlie Sifford
6. Rafer Johnson
7. Larry Doby, Cleveland
8. Arthur Ashe
9. Fritz Pollard, Hammond, in the early 1920s

29.

1. Buddy Werner
2. Jean-Claude Killy
3. Penny Pitou and Betsy Snite
4. Torger Tokle
5. Nancy Greene

30.

1-s, 2-p, 3-r, 4-o, 5-c, 6-k, 7-q, 8-f, 9-l, 10-i, 11-g, 12-h, 13-d, 14-j, 15-b, 16-e, 17-a, 18-m, 19-n

31.

1. Bobby Jones
2. Francis D. Ouimet
3. Jack Westland was forty-seven when he won in 1952
4. Deane Beman
5. Catherine Lacoste
6. Harvie Ward
7. Glenna Collett Vare
8. Dick Chapman
9. Don Cherry
10. John Goodman, 1933

32.

1. Willie Hoppe
2. Eddie Lee
3. Jacob Schaefer, Jr.
4. Ralph Greenleaf
5. Welker Cochran
6. Willie Mosconi

33. a

34.

1. Reginald "Hooley" Smith
2. Jean Beliveau
3. Syl Apps
4. Jack Walker
5. George Hainsworth
6. Max Bentley
7. Nels Stewart
8. Eddie Shore
9. Frank Boucher
10. Frankie Brimsek

35.

1. Ralph Branca, Brooklyn
2. Tom Zachary
3. Vic Raschi, St. Louis
4. Tracy Stallard, Boston Red Sox
5. Warren Spahn, Boston Braves

36.

1-c, 2-d, 3-e, 4-a, 5-b

37.

1. Oregon beat Duke, 20-16, at Durham, N.C.
2. Washington & Jefferson
3. Frank Aschenbrenner
4. Alabama, 1926
5. Ron Vander Kelen and Pat Richter
6. Southern California 29, Washington 0
7. Sandy Stephens
8. Al Carmichael
9. Bob Schloredt

38.

1. Murray Weir, Iowa; Jim McIntyre, Minnesota; Ed Macauley, St. Louis; Ralph Beard, Kentucky; Kevin O'Shea, Notre Dame
2. Walter Dukes, Seton Hall; Bob Houbregs, Washington; Tom Gola, LaSalle; Johnny O'Brien, Seattle; Ernie Beck, Pennsylvania

3. Tony Lavelli, Yale, 1949; Ernie Beck, Pennsylvania, 1953; Chet Forte, Columbia, 1957; Bill Bradley, Princeton, 1964 and '65
4. Wallace Jones, Alex Groza, Ralph Beard
5. Mark Workman, 1952; Rod Hundley, 1956; Jerry West, 1959
6. Bob Cousy, Holy Cross; Kevin O'Shea, Notre Dame; Paul Unruh, Bradley; Paul Arizin, Villanova; Dick Schnittker, Ohio State
7. Guy Rodgers, Temple; Don Hennon, Pittsburgh
8. Bob Pettit, Louisiana State; Cliff Hagan, Kentucky
9. Temple's Bill Mlkvy
10. Cazzie Russell, Michigan; Clyde Lee, Vanderbilt; Dave Schellhase, Purdue; Dave Bing, Syracuse; Louis Dampier, Kentucky

39.

1. Earl Anthony
2. Steve Nagy
3. Don Carter
4. Dotty Fothergill
5. Bill Knox
6. George Young
7. Marion Ladewig
8. Nelson Burton, Jr.
9. Wayne Zahn
10. Floretta McCutcheon

40.

1. Basketball
2. Baseball

3. Football and basketball
4. Football
5. Wrestler
6. Basketball
7. Football and basketball
8. A professional golfer
9. Tennis
10. Major league baseball player

41.

1. Gorgeous George
2. Lou Thesz
3. Lord Carlton
4. Antonio "Argentina" Rocca
5. Big Daddy Lipscomb and Gino Marchetti
6. Gene Stanlee
7. Primo Carnera
8. Vern Gagne
9. Mr. Moto
10. Stanlislaus Zbyszko
11. Buddy Rodgers
12. Woody Strode

42.

1. Lou Gehrig
2. Rocky Graziano
3. Jimmy Piersall
4. Glenn Davis and Doc Blanchard
5. Barney Ross
6. Dizzy Dean
7. Jack Johnson
8. Brian Piccolo

43.

1-i, 2-g, 3-e, 4-j, 5-h, 6-a, 7-c, 8-f, 9-b, 10-d

44.

c

45.

1. Patty Berg
2. Mickey Wright
3. Catherine Lacoste
4. Babe Didrikson Zaharias
5. Glenna Collett Vare
6. Faye Crocker
7. Marlene Hagge
8. Glenna Collett Vare, Helen Hix, Virginia Van Wie, Maureen Orcutt, Mrs. O. S. Hill, and Mrs. L. D. Cheney
9. Mickey Wright
10. Carol Mann

46.

1. Bill Russell, Bob Cousy, Bill Sharman, Tom Heinsohn, Arnie Risen, Andy Phillip, Jim Loscutoff, Frank Ramsey, and Jack Nichols
2. George King's
3. Elgin Baylor of Los Angeles, vs. Boston, April 14, 1962
4. Johnny Moore, San Antonio, April 27, 1983
5. George Mikan, Jim Pollard, Vern Mikklesen,

Slater Martin, Andy Ferrin, Tony Jaros, Bob Harrison, Herm Schaeffer, Don Carlson, Billy Hassett

6. Jack Toomey, Baltimore, vs. New York, committed eight fouls

7. St. Louis: Bob Pettit, Cliff Hagan, Chuck Share, Ed Macauley, Slater Martin, Jack Coleman, Walt Davis, Jack McMahon, Med Park, Win Wilfong

Philadelphia: Wilt Chamberlain, Hal Greer, Luke Jackson, Chet Walker, Wally Jones, Billy Cunningham, Larry Costello, Dave Gambee, Bill Melchionni, Matt Goukas

8. Bob Cousy, vs. Syracuse, March 21, 1953

47.

1. Rick Barry
2. Bill, Barclay, and Bob Plager
3. Johnny and Eddie O'Brien
4. Alex and Ron Johnson
5. Billie Jean Moffit King and Randy Moffit
6. Bruce and Brian Taylor
7. Tom and Dick Van Arsdale
8. Press and Pete Maravich
9. Mike and Marlin McKeever
10. Christy and Henry Mathewsen

48.

1-k, 2-m, 3-o, 4-q, 5-s, 6-t, 7-r, 8-p, 9-n, 10-a, 11-c, 12-e, 13-g, 14-i, 15-j, 16-l, 17-b, 18-d, 19-f, 20-h

49.

1. Detroit Red Wings beat the Montreal Canadiens
2. Toronto Maple Leafs beat the New York Rangers
3. Toronto and Montreal
4. Philadelphia's Bernie Parent, 1974, 1975
5. New York Rangers over the Montreal Maroons
6. Modere Bruneteau of Detroit against the Montreal Maroons
7. Toronto beat Detroit
8. Boston, 1956; Toronto, 1960
9. Toronto
10. Montreal Canadiens beat the Chicago Black Hawks

50.

1. Georgetown vs. North Carolina
2. Gene Tunney outpoint Jack Demsey
3. Billy Jean King vs. Bobby Riggs
4. Harlem Globetrotters, 1951
5. San Francisco 49ers vs. Los Angeles Rams at the L.A. Coliseum
6. Tony Zale's knockout of Billy Pryor

51.

1. Bobby Thompson
2. Moe Drabowsky
3. Elmer Valo
4. Masanori Murakami
5. Reno Bertoia

6. Joe Christopher
7. Andre Rodgers
8. Mike Lum
9. Al Campanis
10. Art Jorgens
11. Jimmy Austin

52.

1. Wilt Chamberlain, Philadelphia, 1967-68
2. Kevin Porter, New Jersey Nets vs. Houston, February 24, 1978
3. Isiah Thomas, Detroit, 1984-85
4. Louis Dampier, Kentucky
5. Dutch Dehnert
6. John Havlicek, Boston
7. Don Buse, Indiana, 1975-76
8. Larry Brown, Denver vs. Pittsburgh, February 20, 1972
9. Oscar Robertson, Cincinnati, 1960-61
10. Bob Davies, vs. Boston, January 22, 1955

53.

1. Gar Wood
2. Chuck Thompson
3. James Thompson
4. Bill Muncey

54. a

55.

1. Jay Berwanger, Chicago, 1935
2. California vs. Pennsylvania, 1951
3. Bobby Grier, Pittsburgh, 1956
4. Houston 24, Los Angeles 16
5. All-Stars 0, Chicago Bears 0
6. Notre Dame's Gus Dorais to Knute Rockne
7. Alabama
8. Willie Thrower, Chicago Bears, 1953
9. Harold Muller, end, California
10. George Connor

56.

1. Stan Mikita
2. Pentti Lund
3. Charlie Gardiner
4. Walt Tkaczuk
5. Wilfred Cude
6. Johnny Gottselig
7. Jimmy McFadden
8. James Conacher
9. Tommy Anderson

57.

1-g, 2-e, 3-a, 4-h, 5-j, 6-i, 7-d, 8-f, 9-c, 10-b

58.

1. Billy Martin
2. Edgar "Sam" Rice
3. Sal Maglie
4. Eddie Collins
5. Gene Bearden

59.

1. Don Schollander
2. Arne Borg
3. Bill Yorzyk
4. Chet Jastremski
5. Mike McDermott
6. Jon and Ilsa Konrads
7. Norman Ross
8. Henry Sullivan
9. George Breen
10. Alan Ford

60.

1. Holy Cross and CCNY
2. Frank McGuire
3. Hank Luisetti
4. Brigham Young
5. North Carolina, 1957 and 1982; North Carolina State, 1974 and 1983, and, to be geographically technical, Georgetown, 1984 and 1985.

61.

1. Tony Esposito, 1969-70
2. Jimmy McFadden
3. Nels Stewart
4. Gus Bodnar
5. Danny Grant, Minnesota North Stars
6. Frank Mahovlich
7. Mike McMahon, 1943-44; Gus Mortson, 1946-47; Barclay Plager, 1967-68; Keith Magnuson, 1969-70
8. Frankie Brimsek, 1939; Terry Sawchuk, 1951; Roger Crozier, 1965; Tony Esposito, 1970; Don Dryden, 1972; Tom Barrasso, 1984
9. 7 goals, 15 assists, 22 points
10. Howie Meeker

62.

1. Bobo Holloman, St. Louis Browns
2. Harvey Haddix, Pittsburgh, vs. Milwaukee, 1959, 35
3. Rudy York, Detroit, August, 1937
4. Bill Wambsganss, Cleveland, 1920
5. Ted Williams, Boston, was forty years old
6. Charley Robertson, Chicago White Sox, 1922
7. J. Owen Wilson
8. Phil Niekro, August 4, 1979
9. Alvin Dark, Boston Braves, 1948
10. Ray Schalk

63.

1. Paul Krause, 1964-79
2. Darrell Royal
3. Erich Barnes
4. Lynn Chadnois
5. Dick "Night Train" Lane
6. Al Simmons
7. Sammy Baugh
8. Al Brosky
9. George Halas' (when playing for the Chicago Bears, Halas went 98 yards with a recovered fumble against Marion on November 4, 1923)
10. George Shaw

64.

A-5-h, B-7-e, C-9-a, D-10-g, E-8-i, F-3-j, G-4-f, H-1-b, I-6-c, J-2-d

65.

1. Cleveland's Bob Feller, vs. White Sox, in Chicago, April 16, 1940
2. Cincinnati Reds
3. Mel Ott, No. 511
4. Chuck Tanner
5. Babe Ruth
6. Walter Johnson, Washington

66. b

67.

1. Pittsburgh Steelers
2. Philadelphia Eagles
3. Chicago Bears, 23, New York Giants 21
4. Chicago Bears when team was located in Decatur, Ill.
5. New York Giants, Dallas Cowboys
6. December 3, 1950, Cleveland vs. Philadelphia
7. Chicago Bears beat the Portsmouth Spartans, 9-0, December 18, 1932
8. Green Bay 37, New York Giants 0, at Green Bay
9. Paul Hornung, Green Bay; Alex Karras, Detroit
10. Alan Ameche, Baltimore, scored a touchdown against the New York Giants

68.

1. None
2. Elgin Baylor, Bob Pettit, Jerry West, and Oscar Robertson
3. Hal Greer
4. Oscar Robertson and Bob Pettit
5. Bob Cousy, 1956 & 1961; Rick Barry, 1966 & 1978
6. Bobby Wanzer, Ed Macauley, Paul Seymour, Fred Schaus, Gene Shue, Richie Guerin, Larry Costello, Bill Sharman, Tom Heinsohn, Billy Cunningham, Lenny Wilkens
7. Wilt Chamberlain
8. Bob Pettit
9. Rick Barry
10. Oscar Robertson

69.

1. Randy Jones, 1974
2. Dick Fowler
3. Claude Passeau
4. Rick Reuschel
5. Christy Mathewson
6. Milt Gaston and Hal Newhouser, respectively
7. Bob Lemon
8. Whitey Ford
9. Allie Reynolds and Larry Gura, respectively
10. Jim Kaat

70.

1. Bill Freehan, Detroit
2. Jerry Grote, New York Mets
3. Frank Hayes
4. Yogi Berra, New York Yankees
5. Ray Schalk
6. John Roseboro
7. Jerry Grote, New York Mets
8. Johnny Edwards, 1970-71
9. Ray Katt
10. Edward J. "Ebba" St. Clair, August 9, 1951

71.

1. Johnny Neun
2. Wes Parker, .9956
3. Ferris Fain

4. Walter Holke
5. Gil Hodges
6. Bill White, 1961, and Jim Bottomley, 1936, respectively
7. Dolf Camilli, Phillies, 1935; Al Oliver, Pirates, 1969; George Metkovich, Red Sox, 1945; Tommy McCraw, White Sox, 1968
8. Bob Robertson
9. Jim Spencer
10. Fred Merkle

72.

1. Red Schoendienst
2. Bobby Knoop
3. Jerry Adair
4. Frankie Frisch, Giants and Cardinals, 42
5. Bill Wambsganss
6. Jim Gilliam
7. Rob Wilfong, Minnesota, .9948, 1980
8. Nap Lajoie
9. Ken Hubbs
10. Gerry Priddy, Detroit; Bill Mazeroski, Pittsburgh

73.

1. Eddie Yost
2. Ray Boone
3. Ron Santo
4. Don Money, Milwaukee
5. Jim Davenport, 1966-68
6. Pinky Higgins

7. Frank "Home Run" Baker
8. Gil Macdougald, N.Y. Yankees, 1951 and John Castino, Minnesota, 1980; Richie Allen, Philadelphia Phillies, 1964; Tommy Helms, Cincinnati, 1966, and Bob Horner, Atlanta, 1978
9. Ron Santo, Cubs, September 3, 1963; Jose Pagan, Pirates, August 18, 1966; Jim Lefebvre, Dodgers, April 25, 1967; Darrell Evans, Giants, April 11, 1980, and Hubie Brooks, Mets, May 10, 1981
10. Pie Traynor

74.

1. Ron Hansen, Washington, July 30, 1968
2. Bert Campaneris, 1970
3. Phil Rizzuto, New York Yankees, 52
4. Rabbit Maranville
5. Mickey Stanley
6. Roger Peckinpaugh
7. Lou Boudreau, .9725
8. Bobby Wine
9. Buddy Kerr
10. Luis Aparicio

75.

1. Pete Rose, .9916
2. Don Demeter, 1962-65
3. Dom DiMaggio
4. Tris Speaker, 1907-28
5. Andy Pafko
6. Ty Cobb
7. Oscar "Hap" Felsch

8. Curt Flood
9. Jose Cardenal
10. Willie Davis

76.

A-5-g, B-6-h, C-8-f, D-10-c, E-11-i, F-9-a, G-4-j, H-2-k, I-3-e, J-1-d, K-7-b

77. b

78.

1. Gertrude Ederle, August 6, 1926
2. Debbie Meyer
3. Ann Curtis, Pat McCormick, Debbie Meyer, and Tracy Caulkins, respectively
4. Ragnhild Hveger
5. Helene Madison
6. Florence Chadwick
7. Aileen Riggin
8. Chris von Saltza
9. Kathy Rawls
10. Shelley Mann

79.

1. Pickles
2. Boo
3. Chico
4. Tex
5. Buddy
6. Skip

7. Crystal
8. Goose
9. Hooks
10. Bevo
11. Dutch
12. Sonny
13. Chick
14. Cotton
15. Houndog

80.

1. Alice Marble
2. Helen Wills
3. Maureen Connolly, 1952-53
4. Margaret Smith Court
5. Elizabeth "Bunny" Ryan
6. Billie Jean King and Rosemary Casals
7. Althea Gibson
8. Gussie Moran
9. Louise Brough and Margaret Osborne du Pont
10. Hazel Hotchkiss Wightman

81.

1-i, 2-g, 3-j, 4-h, 5-a, 6-c, 7-b, 8-d, 9-f, 10-e

82.

1. Frankie Baumholtz
2. Bradley beat Providence, 88-72
3. Ralph Beard's
4. Southern Illinois in 1967

5. Loyola (Chicago)
6. Bill Chmielewski led Dayton past St. John's
7. Byron "Whizzer" White
8. New Mexico
9. Mel Hutchins and Roland "The Cat" Minson
10. St. John's, 1943 and 1944
11. Utah
12. LIU beat Loyola, 44-32
13. George Mikan of DePaul
14. St. Louis

83.

1. Outstanding collegiate football player of the year
2. Leading scorer in the NHL
3. Most Valuable Player in the NBA
4. Outstanding American Amateur Athlete of the year
5. Winner of U.S. vs. Britain in tennis
6. Winner of U.S. vs. Britain, women amateur golfers
7. Winner of world-wide tennis tournament
8. Winner of U.S. vs. Britain, men's professional golf
9. Best pitcher in each major league of baseball
10. Best amateur golf team in the world
11. Champion of the Canadian Football League (professional)
12. National Hockey League Champion
13. Winner of U.S. vs. Britain, men's amateur golf
14. National collegiate football champion
15. Person who has contributed the most to boxing in a year

16. Owner of the horse that wins the steeplechase race at Camden, S.C.
17. Outstanding college or professional football player of the year
18. Outstanding collegiate basketball player of the year

84.

1. Otto Graham, Cleveland, 8.63
2. Jerry Rhome
3. Jim Benton, Cleveland; Cloyce Box, Detroit
4. Billy Stevens
5. Charlie Hennigan, Houston
6. Greg Cook
7. George Blanda, Chicago Bears, Houston, Oakland
8. Dick "Night Train" Lane
9. Don Meredith
10. 1-c, 2-d, 3-a, 4-b

85.

1. Richard Petty
2. Phil Hill
3. Graham Hill
4. Lee Petty
5. A. J. Foyt

86.

1-g, 2-i, 3-f, 4-h, 5-j, 6-d, 7-b, 8-e, 9-c, 10-a

87. c

88.

1-n, 2-l, 3-j, 4-h, 5-b, 6-d, 7-o, 8-m, 9-k, 10-a, 11-c, 12-e, 13-g, 14-i, 15-f

89.

1-d, 2-g, 3-h, 4-j, 5-l, 6-c, 7-k, 8-i, 9-m, 10-a, 11-b, 12-e, 13-f

90.

1. Johnny Blanchard
2. Chuck Essegian
3. Dusty Rhodes
4. J. K. O'Dea
5. Nippy Jones
6. Cookie Lavagetto's

91.

1-e, 2-h, 3-g, 4-i, 5-b, 6-j, 7-f, 8-c, 9-k, 10-d, 11-a

92.

1-f, 2-m, 3-i, 4-n, 5-g, 6-h, 7-e, 8-a, 9-d, 10-l, 11-c, 12-o, 13-b, 14-j, 15-k

93.

1. Lefty Grove
2. Lefty O'Doul
3. Lefty Gomez
4. Lefty Tyler
5. Lefty Williams

94.

1-e, 2-d, 3-f, 4-i, 5-b, 6-j, 7-g, 8-a, 9-c, 10-h

95.

1. Bill Carpenter
2. Joe Bellino
3. Doc Blanchard, Glenn Davis, Dale Hall
4. Tom Hamilton
5. Bob Zastrow
6. Johnny Sai, Pat Donnelly, and Bill Ulrich
7. Tom Cahill
8. Buzz Borries
9. Davis, Blanchard, Joe Stanowicz, John Green, Doug Kenna, Barney Poole
10. Bill Hawkins and Pistol Pete Williams

96.

1. Frank Foss
2. Albert G. Hall
3. Duke Kahanamoku
4. Ethelda Bleibtry
5. Aileen Riggin

97.

1. 1500 meters, 5000 meters, 10,000 meters cross country
2. Ville Ritola
3. Helen Wills
4. Johnny Weissmuller
5. Martha Norelius

98.

1. Elizabeth Robinson
2. Pete Desjardins
3. Percy Williams
4. Ray Barbuti
5. A. B. El Ouafi

99.

1. Luigi Beccali
2. 80-meter hurdles and javelin
3. Eleanor Holm
4. Eddie Tolan
5. Clarence "Buster" Crabbe

100.

1. 100- and 200-meter dashes, long jump, 400-meter relay
2. Jack Lovelock, New Zealand
3. Hill
4. Cornelius Johnson, high jump
5. University of Washington

101.

1. 100-meter dash
2. Fanny Blankers-Koen
3. Emil Zatopek
4. Dr. Sammy Lee
5. Mel Patton edged Barney Ewell

102.

1. Cy Young
2. Herb McKenley, Arthur Wint, Leslie Laing, George Rhoden
3. Pat McCormick
4. Mal Whitfield
5. Horace Ashenfelter

103.

1. Dawn Fraser
2. Ron Delaney
3. Tommy Kono and Paul Anderson
4. Bobby Morrow
5. Murray Rose

104.

1. Abebe Bikila
2. Germany's Armin Hary won the 100 meters; Italy's Livio Berruti won the 200 meters.
3. Wilma Rudolph
4. Chris von Saltza
5. Robert Shavlakadze, U.S.S.R.

105.

1. Donna de Varona
2. Bob Schul and Billy Mills, respectively
3. Fred Hansen
4. Willi Holdorf
5. Bob Hayes

106.

1. Debbie Meyer
2. Al Oerter, discus
3. Vince Matthews, Ron Freeman, Larry James, and Lee Evans
4. Bob Beamon
5. Madeline Manning

107.

1. Wolfgang Nordwig, East Germany
2. Frank Shorter
3. Valery Borzov
4. Balance beam and floor exercise
5. Melissa Belote

108. c

109.

1-c, 2-g, 3-e, 4-i, 5-k, 6-b, 7-j, 8-d, 9-h, 10-l, 11-a, 12-f

110.

1. Rube Marquard
2. Rube Walker
3. Rube Walberg
4. Rube Waddell
5. Rube Benton
6. Andrew "Rube" Foster
7. George "Rube" Foster

111.

1-h, 2-o or k, 3-t, 4-s, 5-m, 6-i, 7-r, 8-p, 9-a, 10-c, 11-e, 12-g, 13-j, 14-q, 15-b, 16-d, 17-f, 18-k or o, 19-l, 20-n

112.

1. Rick Barry
2. Stanley "Stutz" Modzelewski
3. Charley Scott, Virginia, 1971-72
4. Chamberlain, 78 points, against Los Angeles, December 8, 1961
5. Bill Mlkvy
6. David Thompson, Denver, April 9, 1978
7. Newberry
8. Elgin Baylor, 61 points against Boston, April 14, 1962
9. Price Brookfield
10. Wilt Chamberlain
11. Frank Selvy, Furman; Bob Pettit, Louisiana State; Dick Wilkenson, Virginia
12. Bob Kurland

13. Jerry West, 29.1
14. Austin Carr, Notre Dame, 61 in 1970
15. Clyde Lovellette

113.

1-d, 2-e, 3-g, 4-h, 5-i, 6-a, 7-j, 8-c, 9-b, 10-f

114.

1. Chamonix, France, 1924
2. Toni Sailor
3. Dick Button
4. Gretchen Fraser
5. Jack McCartan
6. Hub and Curt Stevens
7. Tenley Albright, 1956
8. John Shea and Irving Jaffee
9. Andrea Mead Lawrence, 1952
10. Edward P. F. Eagan

115.

1-j, 2-g, 3-e, 4-k, 5-i, 6-a, 7-c, 8-f, 9-b, 10-d, 11-h

116.

1. Bobby Bauer, Milt Schmidt, Woody Dumart
2. Sid Abel, Gordie Howe, Ted Lindsay
3. Elmer Lach, Maurice Richard, Toe Blake

4. Joe Primeau, Charlie Conacher, Busher Jackson
5. Bobby Hull, Phil Esposito, Chico Maki
6. Vic Hadfield, Jean Ratelle, Rod Gilbert

117.

1. Roger Bannister
2. Bob Hayes
3. Steeplechase, Horace Ashenfelter
4. Don Bowden, California, 1958
5. Cornelius Warmerdam, 1942
6. Jack Torrance
7. Roland "Gipper" Locke
8. Charlie Dumas
9. Glenn Cunningham
10. John Ulses

118.

1-c, 2-d, 3-b, 4-e, 5-a

119.

1. Chet Walker
2. Earl Monroe
3. Harry Gallatin
4. Oscar Robertson
5. Wilt Chamberlain
6. Billy McGill

120. a

121.

1. Wes Farrell
2. Tony Cloninger
3. Bob Buhl
4. Warren Spahn
5. Bill Hands
6. Lefty Gomez
7. Dave McNally, 1970
8. Dizzy Dean, 1934
9. Mickey Lolich
10. Don Newcombe, 1955; Don Drysdale, 1958 and 1965

122.

1. Andy Seminick and John Boccabella
2. Bill Freehan
3. Johnny Bench, 325, National; Yogi Berra, 313, American
4. Gene Tenace, Oakland, 1972
5. Wes Westrum
6. Ernie Lombardi
7. Elston Howard, Gene Tenace, respectively
8. Johnny Blanchard
9. Roy Campanella
10. Gus Triandos

123.

1. Hank Greenberg, 58, 1938
2. Lou Gehrig, 1934

3. Joe Adcock, 1954
4. George Sisler
5. Johnny Mize, 1947
6. Donn Clendenon, New York Mets
7. Walt Dropo, 1952
8. Jim Bottomley, 1924
9. Jackie Robinson, 1947
10. Lou Gehrig, 493; Willie McCovey, 439, respectively

124.

1. Rogers Hornsby, 1922
2. Bobby Richardson
3. Rogers Hornsby
4. Joe Gordon, 253 career, 32 in 1948
5. Eddie Stankey
6. Dick McAuliffe
7. Joe Gordon and Billy Martin
8. Red Schoendienst, Cardinals
9. Eddie Collins
10. Frankie Frisch
11. Joe Morgan, Cincinnati, 1975, 1976

125.

1. Eddie Mathews, 482
2. Heinie Groh
3. Al Rosen, 1953
4. Brooks Robinson
5. Eddie Mathews and Ron Santo
6. Gil MacDougald

7. Graig Nettles, 319
8. Don Hoak
9. Red Rolfe
10. Fred Lindstrom

126.

1. Arky Vaughn
2. Ed Brinkman, Washington, 1965; Bud Harrelson, New York Mets, 1972
3. Ernie Banks, Chicago Cubs, 293; 47 in 1958
4. Lou Boudreau, 1946
5. Maury Wills, Los Angeles, Pittsburgh, and Montreal
6. Tom Thevenow
7. Phil Rizzuto, New York
8. Rico Petrocelli, 40, 1969; Vern Stephens, 247
9. PeeWee Reese, Brooklyn
10. Eddie Joost, Philadelphia Athletics

127.

1. Hack Wilson
2. Ty Cobb
3. Henry Aaron
4. Bobby Bonds, April 21, 1968
5. Tris Speaker
6. Tommy Holmes, 1945
7. Charlie Keller
8. Roberto Clemente, 1970
9. Babe Ruth, 1928
10. Duke Snider and Lou Brock

128.

1-q, 2-u, 3-e, 4-s, 5-o or t, 6-j, 7-f, 8-t or o, 9-r, 10-b, 11-i, 12-c, 13-h, 14-k, 15-l, 16-a, 17-m, 18-d, 19-p, 20-g, 21-n

129.

1. Larry Kelley and Clint Frank
2. Pete Dawkins, 1968
3. Les Horvath, 1944; Vic Janowicz, 1950; Howard Cassady, 1955, and Archie Griffin, 1974, 1975
4. Dick Kazmaier, 1951
5. Angelo Bertelli, 1943; John Lujack, 1947; Leon Hart, 1949; John Lattner, 1953; Paul Hornung, 1956; John Huarte, 1964
6. Davey O'Brien, TCU, 1938; Doak Walker, SMU, 1948; John David Crow, Texas A&M, 1957; Earl Campbell, Texas, 1977
7. Roger Staubach, Navy, 1963; Archie Griffin, Ohio State, 1974; Billy Simms, Oklahoma, 1978; Herschel Walker, Georgia, 1982
8. Tom Harmon
9. Mike Garrett, 1965; O.J. Simpson, 1968; Charles White, 1979; Marcus Allen, Southern California, 1981
10. Doug Flutie, Boston College

130.

1. Oklahoma A&M
2. Maryland State
3. Texas Western

    4. Tennessee A&I
    5. Alabama Poly

131. c

132.

    1. Anthony Perkins
    2. Dan Dailey
    3. Burt Lancaster
    4. Paul Newman
    5. Jimmy Stewart
    6. Gary Cooper

133.

    1. Dave Philley
    2. Red Ruffing
    3. Dick Williams; Richie Ashburn
    4. Frenchy Bordagaray
    5. Jerry Lynch
    6. Red Schoendienst
    7. Bob Fothergill
    8. Elmer Valo
    9. Johnny Frederick
    10. Ron Northey
    11. Smokey Burgess

134.

1-i, 2-k, 3-m, 4-o, 5-a, 6-c, 7-d, 8-l, 9-n, 10-b, 11-g, 12-f, 13-h, 14-j, 15-e

135.

1. Joe Fulks or Joe Savoldi
2. Joe DiMaggio
3. Joe Namath
4. Joe Walcott
5. Joe Jackson

136.

1. Ed Modzelewski
2. Charley Trippi and John Rauch
3. Glynn Griffing
4. Del Shofner
5. Harry Gilmer
6. Offensive tackle and defensive end Walt Yowarsky
7. Tim Davis
8. Davey O'Brien
9. Charlie O'Rourke
10. Kenny Stabler, quarterback, and Ray Perkins, end

137.

1. Capot
2. Armed
3. Alsab
4. Nashua
5. Seabiscuit

138.

1-h, 2-f, 3-a, 4-b, 5-g, 6-e, 7-d, 8-c

139.

1. Baylor, 1948; Oklahoma A&M, 1949; Kansas State, 1951
2. Ken Heitz, Lynn Shackleford, Lucius Allen, Mike Warren, and Alcindor
3. Bertram H. Born
4. Wisconsin beat Washington State, 39-34
5. Jerry Harkness, Les Hunter, Ron Miller, Vic Rouse, John Egan
6. UCLA
7. Bob Kurland
8. North Carolina State, 1983, 26-10
9. Utah
10. Michigan State and Kansas
11. Texas Western started Bobby Joe Hill, Dave Lattin, Willie Cager, Orsten Artis, and Willie Worsley
12. Hal Lear, Temple
13. Ohio State and Cincinnati
14. Ohio State and Cincinnati, 1961 and 1962

140.

1. 2,434; Clay vs. Liston, May 25, 1965
2. Jersey Joe Walcott was thirty-eight when he lost the title
3. Gene Tunney and Rocky Marciano
4. Tunney vs. Dempsey drew 120,757 in Philadelphia, September 23, 1926
5. Primo Carnera, 6'5¾"
6. Floyd Patterson was twenty-one when he won
7. Spain
8. 63,360; Spinks vs. Ali, September 15, 1978, at the Superdome in New Orleans

9. Primo Carnera at 259½ vs. Paulino Uzcudum at 229, on October 22, 1933
10. Tommy Burns was 5'7"
11. Bobby Fitzsimmons weighed 167 pounds
12. Max Baer, Jim Braddock, Primo Carnera, Max Schmeling, Jack Sharkey

141.

1-t, 2-r, 3-p, 4-n, 5-m, 6-j, 7-a, 8-c, 9-e, 10-s, 11-q, 12-o, 13-b, 14-d, 15-f, 16-h, 17-k, 18-l, 19-i, 20-g

142.

1. Ingemar Johansson
2. Freddy Williamson
3. Brooklyn Dodgers, Chicago Cubs, and Boston Celtics
4. Bernie Casey
5. Muhammed Ali
6. Joe Namath

143. b

144.

1. Jack Nicklaus, 1980
2. Byron Nelson
3. Julius Boros
4. Johnny Miller, 1973; Jack Nicklaus, 1980; Tom Weiskopf, 1980
5. Ray Ainsley
6. Jack Fleck
7. Bobby Jones, 1923, 1929
8. Ben Hogan

9. Francis Ouimet, Jerome Travers, Chick Evans, Bob Jones, and John Goodman

10. In 1947 Snead and Lew Worsham tied at 282, but Worsham won the playoff, 69-70

145.

1-d, 2-l, 3-u, 4-p, 5-k, 6-w, 7-a, 8-s, 9-x, 10-c, 11-y, 12-b, 13-f, 14-t, 15-m, 16-z, 17-e, 18-g, 19-v, 20-q, 21-h, 22-o, 23-i, 24-n, 25-j, 26-r

146.

1. George Woolf
2. Sonja Henie
3. Ed Lewis
4. Tony Lema
5. James Corbett
6. Gil Dodds
7. Reese Tatum
8. Maureen Connolly

147.

1. Dick McGuire
2. Joe Fulks
3. Ed Macauley
4. Jim Loscutoff
5. Rod Hundley

148.

1. East: Boston Patriots, Buffalo Bills, Houston Oilers, New York Titans; West: Dallas

Texans, Denver Broncos, Los Angeles Chargers, Oakland Raiders
2. Tommy Brooker
3. George Blanda and Jim Otto
4. Denver, 13-10
5. Paul Robinson, Cincinnati, 1968
6. Kansas City, 87
7. Denver, 39-97-4
8. Kansas City-Dallas and San Diego-Los Angeles, 48
9. Houston, 70-66-4
10. Boston 63-68-9

149.

1-e, 2-b, 3-h, 4-l, 5-m, 6-c, 7-k, 8-n, 9-a, 10-o, 11-f, 12-g, 13-i, 14-j, 15-d

150.

1. Bob MacKinnon
2. Jim Baechtold
3. Frank Selvy
4. Fred Schaus
5. Howie Dallmar
6. Richie Regan
7. Tom Gola
8. Ernie Calverley
9. Bob Feerick
10. Eddie Conlin

151.

1. Red Grange
2. Wilt Chamberlain

3. Bill Voiselle
4. Jim Otto
5. George Mikan

152.

1-q, 2-u, 3-e, 4-s, 5-t, 6-i, 7-o, 8-n, 9-p, 10-r, 11-a, 12-v, 13-d, 14-m, 15-b, 16-h, 17-j, 18-f, 19-c, 20-g, 21-l, 22-k

153.

1. Glenn Davis
2. Doc Blanchard
3. Elroy Hirsch
4. Albie Booth
5. Charley Justice
6. Roger Staubach
7. O. J. Simpson
8. Howard Cassady
9. Claude Simons
10. Frank Sinkwich

154.

1-c, 2-d, 3-e, 4-a, 5-b

155. b and c

156.

1. Tennessee State, 1957-59; Kentucky State, 1970-72

2. Al Tucker
3. Bob Kauffman
4. Zelmo Beatty
5. Bevo Francis, Rio Grande
6. Willis Reed
7. Bill Riegel
8. Lucious Jackson
9. Earl Monroe
10. Dick Barnett

157.

1. Wally Berger, Boston, 1930; Frank Robinson, Cincinnati, 1956
2. Bob "Hurricane" Hazle
3. Herb Score, 1955
4. George Watkins
5. Ted Williams, Boston Red Sox
6. John Marcum, Philadelphia Athletics, 1933; Dave Ferriss, Boston Red Sox, 1945; Al Worthington, New York Giants, 1953; Karl Spooner, Brooklyn, 1954; Tom Phoebus, Baltimore, 1966
7. Pepper Martin
8. George Scott, Boston, 1966; Larry Hisle, Philadelphia, 1969
9. Tim Raines, Montreal
10. Mike Fornieles, Washington, 1952; Juan Marichal, San Francisco, 1960; Bill Rohr, Boston, 1967

158.

1-s, 2-q, 3-o, 4-m, 5-k, 6-i, 7-t, 8-r, 9-p, 10-n, 11-a, 12-c, 13-e, 14-f, 15-h, 16-j, 17-l, 18-b, 19-d, 20-g

159.

1. Harvey Jackson
2. Modere "Mud" Bruneteau
3. Emile Francis; John Gagnon
4. Clarence "Happy" Day
5. Aubrey "Dit" Clapper
6. Carl Dahlstrom
7. Walter "Babe" Pratt
8. Laurence "Baldy" Northcott
9. Jack Stewart
10. "Sweeney" Schriner

160.

1. Long Jim Barnes
2. Walter Hagan, 1924-27
3. Dow Finsterwald
4. Paul Runyon
5. Bobby Nichols
6. John Golden
7. Jerry Barber, 1961; Don January, 1967; Lanny Wadkins, 1977; John Mahaffey, 1978; David Graham, 1979.
8. No
9. Lionel and Jay Herbert, respectively
10. Gene Sarazen, Leo Diegel, and Denny Shute, respectively

161.

1-f, 2-g, 3-i, 4-h, 5-b, 6-j, 7-d, 8-c, 9-a, 10-e